DIVORCE
IN NEW YORK

DIVORCE IN NEW YORK

> What you need to know about the details of divorce—and how to use mediation and negotiations to cut down on lengthy court battles

Grier H. Raggio, Jr., Lowell K. Halverson, and John W. Kydd

Introduction by
HENRY H. FOSTER, JR., and DR. DORIS JONAS FREED

RUTLEDGE BOOKS

Copyright 1987 by Grier H. Raggio, Jr., Lowell K. Halverson,
and John W. Kydd
All rights reserved

Library of Congress Cataloging-in-Publication Data

Raggio, Grier H., Jr.; Halverson, Lowell K.; Kydd, John W.
Divorce in New York.

Bibliography: p. 213
1. Divorce—Law and legislation—New York (State)
2. Divorce mediation—New York (State)   I. Halverson,
Lowell K.   II. Kydd, John W.   III. Title.
KFN5126.Z9R34   1986   346.74701'66   86-26308
    ISBN 0-87469-060-9 cloth   347.4706166
          0-87469-061-7 paper

Distributed by National Book Network, Inc.
4720 Boston Way, Suite A
Lanham, Maryland 20706

Printed in the United States of America

CONTENTS

CAVEAT	7
PREFACE	9
INTRODUCTION	11
ONE **How to Use This Book**	15
TWO **The Psychological Divorce:** **Putting the Pieces Back Together**	23
THREE **Divorce Mediation: An Alternative**	43
FOUR **Choosing Your Lawyer**	56
FIVE **The Basics of Negotiations**	68
SIX **Property Division**	79
SEVEN **Spousal Maintenance**	100
EIGHT **Child Support**	108

NINE
Child Custody 114
TEN
Joint Custody 124
ELEVEN
Visitation 132
TWELVE
Self-Help 145
THIRTEEN
Cohabitation: Living-Together Arrangements 151
FOURTEEN
Conclusion 165

APPENDIX A
Historical and Policy Overview, by Henry H. Foster, Jr. and Dr. Doris Jonas Freed 167
APPENDIX B
Text: New York State Equitable Distribution Law 178
APPENDIX C
Preparing Financial Information For Your Lawyer 188
APPENDIX D
Child Support Guidelines 203
APPENDIX E
Lawyer Referral Services in New York 206
APPENDIX F
Supreme Courts of New York State 209
APPENDIX G
Resources for Victims of Domestic Violence 211
APPENDIX H
Recommended Reading on Divorce 213

CAVEAT

No BOOK on family law can substitute for the sound judgment and advice of a lawyer dealing with the particular facts of a case.

This book cannot give you legal advice; it can acquaint you with some of the factors lawyers, judges and family counselors consider in resolving marital dissolution disputes. The book is not a do-it-yourself manual for simple or complex divorces. It is a guide to the issues you must resolve in creating the financial, custody and support terms of a divorce agreement. The book also attempts to guide you in choosing an attorney, who will be your essential adviser and employee in navigating through to a negotiated, mediated or litigated result.

PREFACE

THIS BOOK is inspired by and derives from *Divorce in Washington—A Humane Approach* by Lowell K. Halverson and John W. Kydd, published by the Pacific Family Law Institute in Seattle. Lowell, a classmate of mine at Harvard College, suggested that I do a *Divorce in New York* book based on theirs, and I did. I took therapist John Kydd's "psychological divorce" chapter intact from the Washington book, revised the rest for New York law and facts and added materials of my own, including the "negotiations" chapter.

This book discusses three models for resolving the custody, property, and support issues that often occur at the end of marriage: adversary litigation in court, settlement through negotiations, and settlement through mediation. The models overlap, and a court fight, negotiations between the parties' attorneys, and direct exchanges between husband and wife assisted by a mediator may each be appropriate at different stages of a case. The authors' recommendation, based on experiences as divorce attorneys, is against full-scale litigation and courtroom trials. The litigation process is slow, painful, and often a waste of the spouses' financial and emotional resources. A bitter divorce may also irrevocably damage a parent's relationship with his or her children. Both husband and wife must be willing and able to reach a common ground if negotiations are to succeed.

If the spouses are to avoid adversary litigation, they should negotiate or mediate being mindful of the standards for property division, custody, and support that New York courts would apply were the parties to go to trial. Those standards are a public definition of what is "fair" and serve as guidelines for negotiated or mediated settlements. Much of this book therefore discusses those rules as embodied in New York's Equitable Distribution Law.

We especially wish to thank Professor Henry H. Foster, Jr.; Dr. Doris Jonas Freed; H. Miles Jaffe; Sandra C. Katz; Lenard Marlow; Kenneth Neumann; Loraine A. Gruber; Fred Sammis; Faigy Friedman; Allan Mogel; Evelyn Fiore; Harriet R. Ripinsky; Linda Ripinsky; Leo Kayser, III; Robert J. Franklin; Harold Matson; Joan Fulton; and Louise, Lorraine, and Julie Raggio for their help and comments on drafts of this book.

Grier H. Raggio, Jr.
February, 1987
New York, New York

INTRODUCTION

THIS BOOK provides a roadmap for one traveling through the divorce process. It is written in plain English for divorce clients and their families and friends. It avoids "legalese," gives examples, and provides an accurate account of the divorce process which often appears meaningless to the layman. Clients, lawyers, mental health professionals, and the general public will benefit from reading it. New York lawyers will find the book helpful to those of their clients who are struggling with the shocks of separation. It offers much insight and information to help them endure the trauma of divorce.

The strength of this book is that it concentrates on the human, psychological and economic problems involved in divorce and at the same time clarifies the legal problems. Grier Raggio, the co-author we know best, is an experienced matrimonial and trial lawyer who cares for people and effectively advances his clients' long-term best interests. He is a proponent of planning for the future and working with the present rather than fighting about the past. He is dedicated to protecting the welfare of the children of divorce, who are too often the real sufferers when their parents go to court.

The book provides essential knowledge on property distribution upon divorce, maintenance, child support, custody, and visitation in understandable language for the lay reader. Mr. Raggio discusses such hotly contested issues as joint custody and has added an interesting chapter on the legal rights of nonmarital partners or cohabitants.

Those rules are discussed here in a practical and realistic way as knowledge the divorcing person needs to participate in settling his or her own divorce problems. There is more emphasis on what goes on behind the scenes in solving those problems than about technical rules applicable to divorce trials, such as the rules of legal procedure and the grounds of divorce in New York. The latter are mentioned, but Mr. Raggio is chiefly concerned with the divorce process as it takes place in real life and in the personal experiences of clients. For many years over ninety percent of New York divorces have been "uncontested." This means that only one party actually shows up in court, and usually there is a ritual inquest with stock questions and answers that may take all of ten minutes. The practical significance of the over nine-to-one ratio of divorce cases that are resolved without a court trial over those that are tried cannot be ignored.

This reality means that for middle and upper income clients it is the *negotiation* process that is pivotal: "bargaining leverage" may be crucial. Chapter Five gives an insight into the negotiation process and advises the client to concentrate upon what he or she *most* wants and to be prepared to give ground on what the other party *most* wants. Informed predictions of what a court would do in the facts of your case, if there were a trial, often sets limits for negotiation. Mr. Raggio has had considerable experience in negotiation as well as trial work. In passing, it may be of interest that he comes from a family of lawyers. His mother, Louise Raggio of Dallas, is a past chairperson of the Family Law Section of the American Bar Association and remains active in its affairs. His father and two brothers practice in Dallas, and are well-known family lawyers. Matrimonial law for the Raggios has been a family specialty.

Of deep concern to Mr. Raggio is the rapidly developing alternative of divorce mediation, in which the parties negotiate directly, with the assistance of a trained mediator, and use their attorneys as advisers and draftsmen rather than as gladiators. Mr. Raggio gives the pros and cons of mediation as a way of reaching a divorce settlement and warns of some of its dangers, but obviously favors mediation for those clients where he believes it will work. His working assumption is that divorce is at the same time the legal killing of a marriage and the start of a new legal, social, and economic relationship between the former spouses. The new relationship is particularly important if there are young children, for the divorced parents will be sharing financial and nurturing responsibilities for their children, attending the same school plays, athletic events, graduations, and weddings for many years. A long, bitter divorce process in which the parties do not come to terms with the resentments and regrets they each carry from the marriage will be a continuing poison in that new relationship; conversely, a mediated settlement may be the best start for that new relationship.

Whether mediation is appropriate or not, one of the most helpful features of this book is that it places divorce in the broad context of a person's life and relates the process to short-term and long-term objectives. A client will learn why it is to his or her best interest to bury hostility along with the dead marriage, and to constructively plan for the future.

The client who enters the divorce process should be aware of the possible and the probable. Emotionally mature couples have always been able to agree and reach an amicable settlement, with or without the aid of lawyers or mediators. But that civilized behavior is all too rare, and the divorce process often brings out the worst in people, unless the client has listened to a lawyer like Mr. Raggio, who takes a "planning for the future" approach. What the trade calls "bomber" lawyers are easily available; and when a client deliberately chooses a bomber the flak begins, things heat up, bitterness and hostility are intensified, and divorce becomes a life-and-death struggle with no holds barred. Sometimes the bomber snows under his adversary with tons of paper work, motions, depositions, interrogatories, and the like, in the hope of getting the victim to cry "uncle." Whether the bomber achieves his or her immediate goal or not, inevitably the legal expenses skyrocket and the parties and their children all suffer heavy emotional and psychological casualties.

It need not be that way. From this book you may learn that there are alternatives to a cat-and-dog fight in court where all the dirty linen is exposed and anger is vented. You and your spouse may be fortunate enough to engage attorneys who "cool it" and plan and negotiate effectively for your and your children's futures. Or, you and your spouse may be mature and rational enough to go the mediation route using attorneys only as advisers and draftsmen. Hopefully, the tools available in this book will assist you and your spouse to shape your divorce result rather than leaving the job mostly to lawyers and to judges. Even if litigation is necessary, this book can help you in preparing your case and in formulating your long-term goals after divorce. With help and luck you can endure the trauma of the divorce process and become a better person for the experience. As Grier Raggio suggests, set your eyes on the future and bury the past and get on with it so you may make a fresh start. As some of us know, life is too short to be wasted in a running battle to get the better of the person you once loved and who is the parent of your children. Shalom!

Henry H. Foster, Jr.
Professor of Law Emeritus
New York University

Doris Jonas Freed, S.J.D.
New York, New York

February, 1987

CHAPTER ONE

HOW TO USE THIS BOOK

THIS BOOK is written for any person who, even for a fleeting instant, has thought about getting a divorce. The reality is that one of every two marriages in America ends in divorce. We want to give you information and concepts while you and your spouse are talking civilly (and perhaps we can even help keep your marriage alive). Once a husband and wife begin trading blows through lawyers, it is difficult to reverse the process. If they do not back away from their particular abyss, the spouses are due for unnecessarily painful and scarring experiences. We write also for mothers-in-law, brothers, best friends, and others who become emotionally involved in the divorce process.

There are two basic themes in this book. The first is that a fight in court is often a disastrous way to end a marriage. The second is that husbands and wives should try to take charge themselves of creating the essential financial and custody terms of their separation and divorce, once it is clear that their marriage is over. With the marriage dead and at least one spouse hurting and bitter, starting a court battle may seem the natural thing to do. For the hurt spouse to negotiate rather than litigate requires maturity. We argue that it is worth it. We encourage spouses to participate actively in formulating the financial, custody, and support terms of their divorce arrangement. We also offer help in choosing the right attorney to help you through to a negotiated, mediated, or litigated settlement. The book's sections on New York law are tools for you to use in evaluating the reasonableness and fairness of any proposed solutions to the specific custody, support, and property division questions in your case. Some of those tools you may not need; for instance, there may be no children, so the child custody portions of the book can be ignored. The entire thrust of the book is to assist you in ending your marriage, if it should be ended, on terms that will best allow you to move forward with your life.

In law school, students read cases reporting how judges decide specific disputes. The idea is to learn general principles by studying specific applications. Thus, we have created a divorcing couple, Mary Ellen and Jim, using our experiences to illustrate frequent issues in divorce cases. In our example, the wife is the economically dependent homemaker and the husband the dynamic businessman. This is not meant to be sexist, but is simply a reflection of a common arrangement. Obviously there are couples where the wife makes the money and the husband has the bulk of child care responsibilities.

MAYBE IT'S OVER . . . WHERE DO I GO FROM HERE?

Mary Ellen sat down across the desk, forcing a smile. It was obvious that she felt uneasy visiting an attorney—not unlike many of the clients we have seen in our office over the past several years. After sixteen years, her marriage was not what she and her husband wanted it to be, yet she was not sure a divorce was what she wanted either. We have to be candid with our clients: we're lawyers, not marriage counselors. We can advise prospective clients about the *legal* aspects of divorce, but we cannot advise them whether or not they *should* dissolve their marriage. When a client is uncertain or fearful, clarification of the legal and psychological issues involved frequently can help them to make the dissolution decision.

Mary Ellen needed to know about emotional and legal consequences of a divorce action and had taken the giant first step of coming to a lawyer. She didn't need to feel alone. In 1984, there were about 1,200,000 marital dissolutions granted in the United States.

"I'm not here because of wifebeating or alcoholism. Basically, Jim and I just grew apart. Everyone thinks we're the all-American family. Justin is fourteen, and Kristin's eleven. Jim and I are proud of our family.

"We're also proud of what we've achieved. I don't really know where to start. We've worked so hard and it just now appears to be paying off. Jim has really accomplished a lot; I was alongside him every inch of the way. He has a MBA. I guess I feel it's my degree too, because I put him through school during the first years of our marriage. I taught high school English in Boston. We lived on my income. That made me feel important.

"We came back to New York City fourteen years ago. Jim got the MBA, and I produced Justin. I haven't worked since then, at least not for pay. Oh, I've spent many, many hours working in the kids' schools and doing other volunteer work, but I haven't had a *real* job. I guess I believed my duty was to be a good wife and mother, so I never even updated my teaching credentials.

"Anyhow, after we moved back home, Jim got a good job heading the marketing research department of a pharmaceutical firm. He stayed there for five years and then, nine years ago, he and two other fellows from the company started their own business. They formed a corporation that designs and produces medical supplies. Jim is responsible for the sales end of the operation. Now it's really starting to go, but I sure was frightened in the beginning. The loan we needed to start the business seemed overwhelming. For six months Jim did not draw a salary. We lived off our savings.

"Actually, it really didn't take that long for the business to get off the ground. Six years ago we were able to buy our present home. Of course, we had the profit from the sale of our first home to help with the down payment, but at the time it seemed like a huge financial commitment.

"So over the years, we grew into a comfortable lifestyle, but when you strip away all our material possessions, there isn't much left. Of course, we have the kids, but aside from them, it gets awfully lonely in this marriage. Jim and I can barely agree on the time of day anymore. In fact, I'm just now recognizing all the subtle put-downs Jim has been handing me over these last years. Now I see how his put-downs have been eating away at my self-esteem, and the crazy part is that Jim still isn't even aware of what he has done. What I'm saying is that we aren't good for one another anymore.

"What is right for us, all of us, including the children? Kristin needs braces—you know what that costs. Justin was just accepted into a very expensive private school. I want the kids to have all the advantages. What will a divorce do to their well-being?"

Mary Ellen continued with some specific questions:

"The kids are used to our home. Do you think I could keep it? Even if I can keep it, how can I afford to live there, or anywhere else for that matter? I haven't worked for so long; I really don't know that I could get a job. Besides, women just don't seem to earn that much money.

"If we both want a divorce, does that mean that I'm entitled to 'alimony'? How about the kids? Who'll pay for Kristin's braces and Justin's schooling, not to mention college, clothes, doctor bills, soccer shoes?

"If Jim moves out, what will I do for money? What if he won't leave? Am I forced to move out? Will we end up hating each other? Does every divorce have to be ugly?

"How will our kids behave? Our divorced friends' kids turn into monsters, especially when they bring home new 'friends'. I'm just assuming I would have custody of the children. Doesn't the mother always get custody?

"How do you start a divorce? Can Jim and I both use the same lawyer? How long does it take? It seems as though all our friends' divorces dragged on *forever*.

"I guess I'm just overwhelmed. Jim and I are unhappy in our marriage, but neither of us is sure that divorce wouldn't make a worse mess of our lives."

There aren't "yes" and "no" answers to all of Mary Ellen's questions. Speaking generally, one could say "yes, you may get the house; yes, you probably will need to become employed; and we'll make provisions for the children in the settlement agreement." But each divorce situation is unique, and a court or negotiating attorneys must consider many factors, including the age, income, and future earning capacity of the spouses. In settling the financial terms of divorce, every asset and liability of the parties has to be looked at. Few divorcing spouses will maintain their current standard of living with two households to support and not necessarily more income.

What will Mary Ellen do for money if Jim moves out? The courts make provisions for this. You will find an explanation of "temporary relief" in Chapter Seven, "Spousal Maintenance." In fact, as this book progresses, it is our intention to answer all of Mary Ellen's questions and also the questions Jim has asked his attorney.

In answer to the question about both spouses employing the same attorney, in general an attorney should not represent clients on both sides of a conflict, since practically every marital dissolution involves conflicting interests between husband and wife. New York State's highest court, however, has ruled that an agreement that divided the spouses' property and settled custody and support would be enforced if its terms were fair, even though the attorney who drafted the agreement represented both husband and wife. A properly trained attorney can act as a mediator for both parties, and some attorney-mediators also draft the agreement that emerges from the mediation. If your agreement is drafted by someone who is not exclusively your attorney, I suggest that you have your own attorney review it before you sign.

Although men and women at the end of a traditional marriage face different factual problems, they often suffer from the same divorce-induced emotional problems. While my female clients may fear that they will not be able to survive economically, my male clients often fear losing their home, losing contact with their children, and losing many of their assets in a divorce court they suspect is biased in favor of women. Again, in some marriages, the sex roles are reversed, or just different from the "traditional" marriage. Anger, guilt, hostility, anxiety, failure, rejection—these emotions don't favor men or women. Unwinding the legal relationship between spouses, although important, is usually only one act in a larger drama with many emotional scenes. John Kydd, who is a therapist as well as a matrimonial attorney, summarizes specific stages of emotional recovery in Chapter Two, "The Psychological Divorce."

Clients often need both legal and psychological advice. We regularly recommend counseling to clients who might benefit from it. Because Mary Ellen was not convinced that a divorce was the answer to her problems, that is what we did in her case. It is always wise to explore the alternatives before committing to divorce.

Most nonviolent couples should attend counseling sessions together because counseling involves three entities: the man, the woman, and the marriage. Patterns are evident when the couples attend together which are absent when they see the counselor separately. Couples who are able to go to counseling together are actually more likely to remain together. But even if these couples do dissolve their marriage, they often have an easier time of it because counseling teaches them to communicate better with one another. If they are communicating, they can cooperate.

After three months of counseling, Mary Ellen scheduled an appointment to start the marital dissolution process. She had learned that she felt too much hurt and anger to stay successfully in the marriage. The counseling had helped clarify the problems; Mary Ellen was convinced now of the need to end her marriage.

Making the divorce decision did not prevent Mary Ellen from having strong and sometimes frightening feelings about the end of her marriage.

> "I feel guilty, and then I feel angry about the guilt, and angry at Jim because he never understood my needs. I know I want out, but still I feel a sense of failure. Why couldn't I make it work? Is it my fault? I thought my kids would be on my side, but they've really been very difficult. Justin is surly; he seems to always be angry with me. Kristin has become withdrawn and irresponsible."

Mary Ellen was clearly in the early stages of the psychological divorce process. She was startled but relieved to learn that she was fitting into a very normal pattern. We promised her that this phase would pass—and emphasized that right now we had work to do. Prior to this meeting, we had sent her a large packet of preparatory materials which she was to complete and bring with her. She was to gather specific information regarding all the tangible assets and liabilities accumulated during the marriage. We needed this in order to prepare what is known as a Verified Complaint for Divorce. We explained to Mary Ellen that a summons, usually along with a Verified Complaint, starts the divorce process in New York. The complaint includes provisions for child custody, visitation rights, support, and the division of property and debts.

Whatever your own situation, it will have similarities to the circumstances in Mary Ellen's case and certainly will have its own peculiarities. Divorce issues vary as much as people do. It is not practical to make an attempt to discuss them all. This book has been designed so that you can do much of the preparatory work yourself. As you work through each chapter you will gain knowledge and confidence. Reading of possible solutions to some of the legal and economic problems, you will begin to solve the psychological puzzles of your own particular situation.

For instance, Chapter Two, "The Psychological Divorce: Putting the Pieces Back Together," helps you understand your feelings and directs you in ways to turn negative thoughts into a positive outlook so that you can begin creating a new life.

Chapter Three, "Divorce Mediation: An Alternative," is perhaps the most important of this book. It describes what experience has taught us to consider the most effective way for some couples to proceed with a divorce.

Chapter Four, "Choosing Your Lawyer," is meant to help you decide which lawyer out of the thousands available to you is the best for you in terms of ability, cost, and contribution to your personal comfort level.

Chapter Five, "The Basics of Negotiations," explores the attitudes you will need and suggests some of the tools that will make you effective in negotiating your own divorce settlement.

Chapter Six, "Property Division," sheds light on solving the difficult division of goods and avoiding new anger and hurt.

Chapter Seven, "Spousal Maintenance," deals with one of

Mary Ellen's first concerns: How does she support herself and her children during divorce proceedings?

Chapter Eight, "Child Support," examines another difficult financial aspect.

Chapter Nine, "Child Custody," gives careful guidance toward finding the least harmful solutions.

Chapter Ten, "Joint Custody," continues the discussion.

Chapter Eleven, "Visitation," discusses possible ways to keep this aspect of divorce from breaking down into ugly confrontations.

Chapter Twelve, "Self-Help," is for those who will want to do legal research on their own. For instance, there is in this chapter an explanation of how to use law books.

Chapter Thirteen, "Cohabitation: Living-Together Arrangements," is for those who choose not to (or cannot) be legally married. If you are one, you should be aware of the legal and economic consequences of your way of life.

The Appendices include a historical and policy overview of New York divorce law by Professor Foster and Dr. Freed. Also included are the names and addresses of courts, agencies, and other services that can be called on for help through the rougher aspects of a divorce.

At the end of some chapters there are lists of additional questions. Use these lists, and this entire book, to help you define and begin to solve all the points that apply to your own divorce. But remember that while you will have learned more about the specific aspects of your divorce, no book can substitute for having your own attorney advise you.

CHAPTER TWO

THE PSYCHOLOGICAL DIVORCE: PUTTING THE PIECES BACK TOGETHER

DIVORCE OCCURS in two places: in the court and in your heart. Those who fail to recognize this "divorce of the heart" often fail to learn from the mistakes of their first relationship and are likely to repeat these mistakes in later relationships. This book is about winning both in the court and in the heart. Too many people who win the court battle find that they have lost the war because their family is so shattered by the trial experience that neither parent can adequately function to meet his or her needs or the children's. The bottom line is: bitter divorce battles beget bitter post-divorce battles.

The purpose of this chapter is to help you to win that second divorce battle: the battle to become the best person or parent you can be in spite of the difficulties of your divorce. We believe that clients who learn from the emotional and the legal processes of their divorce also learn how to have more satisfying personal and parental relationships in the future.

Plainly, the psychological process of divorce is critical, and we need lawyers who are trained to deal with the divorce process as a whole, and not just its legal aspects in isolation. Many national organizations are developing new approaches to divorce, which address both the psychological and the legal problems that men and women face. The psychological divorce has stages, just as the legal divorce does. Many clients find struggling with their feelings far more difficult than struggling with the legal process.

For example, late one afternoon John came by the office to see if we could talk. His face was drawn and his cigarette trembled slightly between his fingers. He was usually confident and outspoken, with a "can do" attitude about life. Now his eyes seemed flat and tearful and his voice was unsteady.

> "You know, now that I'm here I don't know where to start. I'm usually pretty much in control and on top of things but somehow . . .
>
> "Anyway, today everything just collapsed. It felt like something in me shifted and my stable self just came down like a house of cards. I had to skip work: this is the first thing I've done today and it's 4:00 P.M.!
>
> "I don't mind telling you this really scares me. For a minute there I thought 'so this is what it's like to have a breakdown.' I'm at the point where my chest actually hurts when I think about the divorce. I always thought that 'heartache' was something in songs, but this really hurts!
>
> "Maybe you're not the right one to talk to about this, but I sure don't want to go to a counselor. All I want to know is how long will this last? I can't stay this empty very long or I'll be out of a job!"

John's feelings are not unique; many men struggle through them without talking about it. Thanks to a growing movement of support groups for men, the situation is improving. Still, we can't begin to count the number of men who haven't come in until after they gave up trying to drink, sweat, or work through their emotional problems themselves. It's an absolute fact that men, like women, have feelings that need special attention and understanding during a divorce. We *all* know that there are identifiable psychological steps or stages in a divorce. Every book on

The Psychological Divorce: Putting the Pieces Back Together 25

divorce has its own particular version of the stages of divorce. We have found Dr. Bruce Fisher's book, *Rebuilding* (Impact Press, 1981), most useful in our practice, so we will use his work here.

STAGES OF DIVORCE RECOVERY

It is a cliché that divorce is a bitter experience that often engenders deep feelings of revenge, retaliation, despair, and disappointment. Many people going through divorce reconsider their basic values towards life. Although many view divorce as a time of disability, self-doubt, and unresolvable fears, divorce is also an opportunity to answer serious questions about how to learn from the past, how to gain self-knowledge, and how to grow from the experience.

The process can be compared to a crab's shedding its old shell to grow a new one. Just before breaking out of its old shell, the crab is very uncomfortable and almost unable to fend for itself because of the extreme pressures that have built up inside the shell. When it finally breaks out, it faces a dangerous world with very little protection. The crab's response is to bury itself deep into the sand for a few weeks until sufficient new armor has built up to make it once again safe to journey into the outside world.

In human terms, the person initiating the divorce often spends a considerable amount of time trapped and cramped inside the old shell of the marriage. Spouses breaking out of their shells often find they are fearful about becoming single adults. Some will bury themselves with work or at home in order to gain time and sufficient self-confidence to reenter society.

One of the underlying themes is: *different people progress at different rates*. Normally, the psychological divorce takes at least one year. Some people begin their psychological divorce long before filing their legal divorce, while others do not begin it until long after their legal divorce is final. Also, there is significant evidence that men and women tend to react differently to the stresses created by divorce. Some men tend to act more *upon the world* as a means of coping, and they do so by working long hours, partying hard, etc. Some women, on the other hand, tend to act more *upon themselves,* and will seek counseling for an inner explanation of the failure of the marriage. Almost twice as many women as men seek early help for personal divorce-related problems. It has been suggested that this means that women are less able to handle their problems without help. Studies in emergency clinics indicate, however, that most men do not seek help until their problems have become acute and require extensive care. Women are likely to seek help earlier and more often and usually overall require *less* care before they are fully recovered.

Lastly, remember that the children of divorce go through similar stages of recovery. Parents should be supportive but must also take care not to spend so much time helping the kids that they avoid dealing with their own problems. What follows is a summary of the stages of divorce recovery.

STAGE 1. DENIAL: FACING UP TO IT

(A) THE INITIAL SHOCK

Traditionally, at our wedding, we promise to be together until "death do us part," and most of us believe that divorce is something that only happens to others. When we suspect that it's happening to us, it is difficult to admit the failure, partly because we fear rejection by our friends. In addition to the stigma of divorce, there is the fear that the fact of divorce means that we will never again have a satisfactory intimate relationship. Given these feelings, isn't it reasonable that many people prefer stunted, cramped marriages over the risks inherent in breaking out of the marital relationship?

Many people spend months trying to find precisely "what went wrong." Sometimes it is easier to get clear answers by asking the question "why were we married?" instead of "why were we divorced?" Take some time for honest inquiry:

- Were you and your partner friends?
- Did you confide in one another?
- Did you share friendships?

The Psychological Divorce: Putting the Pieces Back Together

- Did you go out together socially?
- Did you make major decisions jointly?
- Did you trust each other?
- What interests did you share? Attitudes toward life? Politics? Religion? Children? Hobbies?
- When you got angry with each other, did you deal with it directly, or hide it, or try to hurt each other?

Although these questions may be difficult to ask, thoughtful and honest answers are worth the effort. *Easy explanations of a divorce are usually incorrect.*

It can take weeks or months to work through this stage. The following checklist will help you to decide if you have in fact come through it and are ready to pass to the next stage:

1. I am able to accept that my love relationship is ending.
2. I am comfortable telling my friends and relatives that my love relationship is ending.
3. I have begun to understand some of the reasons why my love relationship did not work out, and this has helped me overcome the feelings of denial.
4. I believe that even though divorce is painful, it can be a positive and creative experience.
5. I am ready to invest emotionally in my own personal growth, in order to become the person I would most like to be.
6. I want to learn to become fulfilled as a single person before committing myself to another love relationship.
7. I will continue to invest in my own personal growth, even if my former love partner and I plan to get back together.

(B) FROM LONELINESS TO ALONENESS

It is natural to feel extreme loneliness when your love relationship ends. Many people have great fear that this utter loneliness will never end and that they would do anything to get their partner to return. Even if the children are living with you and there are friends and relatives nearby, the loneliness is often greater than all of the warm feelings these loved ones have for you. Answers emerge from your feelings.

This step is about learning how to grow *through* loneliness to the state of aloneness, where you are comfortable being by yourself. It begins with a "hiding in sand" period; you may feel that you are safe only so long as you never venture out again.

Some dive into their apartments for weeks at a time, while others dive into their work. Each is an equally effective avoidance that is healthy over a short term, but dangerous over a long term. A variation on this theme is to dive into a rebound relationship, where all the painful unanswered questions of the old relationship are avoided by devoting one's total energy to a new relationship. Such rebound relationships can be extremely exciting and dangerous, especially when relief is mistaken for love.

Getting to a point of "aloneness" involves being comfortable doing things by yourself and for yourself. During the loneliness period, some say that food tastes flat, television is boring, and that it is impossible to read. There is a nagging feeling that you must do *something*, but no clear idea as to what that "something" is. Eventually, the all-pervasive feelings of loneliness simply fade and cease to control your behavior. The need to hide in the sand, in your work, or in the arms of another falls away like an old and outworn shell.

(C) GUILT VERSUS REJECTION: DUMPERS AND DUMPEES

"Dumpers" are those who end the love relationship; "dumpees" have it ended for them. The adjustment process differs, since dumpers tend to feel more *guilt* while dumpees feel more *rejection*. Also, dumpers start their psychological adjustment while still in the love relationship, and dumpees can only start adjusting later. Plainly, the adjustment process is easiest for couples who mutually decide to end their relationship.

The personal "fault" for a divorce is often placed upon the party who starts the lawsuit for divorce. Thus, both parties will often go to great lengths not to initiate the divorce. One party may terminate sexual relations, while the other may move out, yet neither be willing to sue for a divorce. For the dumpee, the divorce papers sometimes come as a surprise, and he/she feels unprepared to face the legal and emotional decisions that the dumper is forcing upon both of them. Frequently the dumpee will plead for delay and may attempt last-minute changes or give up everything, in hope of buying a reconciliation. If this does not work, the dumpee is forced to acknowledge the reality of the divorce. The anger that often builds up along with this realization may create a revengeful cycle of retributive litigation, in the dumpee's attempt to "get even" or to prove he/she is in the right.

While dumpees strive to overcome feelings of rejection and anger, dumpers try to deal with a sense of guilt for terminating the relationship. Many punish themselves as a means of dealing with this guilt. Court settlements frequently are negotiated while dumpers feel so guilty they will give up everything, and while dumpees will settle for anything in hope of getting the dumper back. Some dumpers are willing to give up anything in order to get out of the marriage; and some dumpees are willing to ask for nothing in order to get back together. In terms of individual consciousness, the dumper often wants to work on his relationship with himself (or herself) (e.g., "I need to get out in order to straighten myself out"), while the dumpee wants to work on the relationship with the dumper ("I can't give up on it until I'm sure it's gone forever").

The dumper/dumpee concept helps explain why some children become very angry at the parent who decided to leave. These children often take out the fear, rejection, and frustration they feel on the parent most easily blamed. The children may even be viewed as dumpees because they have very little to do with the divorce decision and often feel the same anger and frustration that dumpees do. In addition, they will often feel responsibility for the entire breakup, imagining that if only they had behaved differently, their parents would not be divorcing. Parents must do their best to maintain a quality relationship with the children during the entire separation and divorce process. Otherwise it is difficult for the children to realize that *they are not guilty* of causing the divorce. Some children carry this stigma of responsibility for their parents' divorce into their own relationships as adults.

(D) GRIEF: BIG BOYS—AND GIRLS—DO CRY

Once you are past the cycle of guilt and rejection you are confronted with the painful reality of the death of your relationship.

The trauma of divorce is quite similar to that of the death of a loved one. According to Elizabeth Kubler-Ross, there are five basic stages in coping with a death:

1. *Denial.* Here there is a feeling of numbness, shock and detachment from the world. Many report feeling and acting like robots.
2. *Anger.* The anger that has been turned inward to build depression now turns outward. The frustrations that have simmered for years in the relationship may suddenly boil over. Clients report that they try to convince anyone within earshot how absolutely horrible their ex-partner was. This is a stage of paradox; as long as the hatred continues, it is difficult to answer why you chose to fall in love in the first place. On the other hand, if you choose to maintain that he/she was a splendid person, then honestly expressing anger is difficult.
3. *Bargaining.* The bereaved feel that they would do anything to have the lost partner's return. This is a very difficult period, when one partner is willing to do anything to keep the marriage going, while the other is likely to feel enormous guilt. Both try for another chance when the relationship is plainly dead. They may come back together for the wrong reasons, such as, deciding to have a child in order to save the marriage.
4. *Letting go.* This is a very depressing stage, when the person finally comes to grips with the reality of facing life without the relationship. Thoughts of suicide are common at this point, but these same thoughts are a marvelous vehicle for asking deep questions about the purpose of one's life, for building a stronger identity, and for finding a deeper and more productive purpose in living.
5. *Acceptance.* Finally the day comes when the grief of the old relationship no longer needs to be carried from day to day. Once the loss is accepted, the burden falls away and there is no more need to invest in a relationship that is past.

Keeping in mind these stages, the sensitive parent will be aware that children go through similar stages. Everyone needs time to cry. Tears are a necessary part of leave-taking, and mood changes may be rapid and surprising. Don't be shocked: you may be meeting new aspects of yourself. Go with the feelings and learn. The only sure way to be stuck in the grief cycle is to refuse to let yourself express the pain you feel. Not only is divorce emotionally similar to bereavement—it can be even more traumatic than the death of a loved one.

Some who have worked through the grief cycle report that their constant depression has stopped, that they have recovered physical and emotional energy to work from morning to night, and that they have little trouble concentrating. In addition, they often report that they have stopped talking about their crisis, that they have no thoughts of attempting suicide, that they eat and live normally, and that they no longer feel that they are operating as robots from day to day.

Please bear in mind that grieving over one relationship also may trigger earlier grief that has not been dealt with. For example, one man reported that he found himself dreaming about the death of his mother when he was a young boy. Such feelings and dreams are important because the more you deal with them, the better able you are to get on with productively pursuing the rest of your life.

(E) ANGER: DAMN THE S.O.B.!

Once the depression cycle is broken, the pent-up anger often rushes out like water through a broken dam. Many people have difficulty letting their anger out, so they remain depressed, while spending much of their energy containing their rage. Basically there are three phases in dealing with anger: the first is to feel it, the second is to express it constructively, and the third is to forgive both yourself and your ex-partner.

The importance of feeling anger is that it creates *distance* from your ex-partner and allows you to function better on your own. Like grief, the anger may come from many sources, and it can only be dealt with to the extent that it is honestly acknowledged.

The second phase is to express the anger constructively. Some spouses report having an active fantasy life in which they dream of letting the air out of the ex-partner's tires, chopping down all the trees around the house, or covering the front walk with banana peels on a foggy morning. Others scream or cry out their anger, and some divert the tremendous anger-created energy to good use by cleaning the house from top to bottom, or doing a great deal of physical exercise. The key point in this phase is that unless you have had a professionally structured experience (with a marriage counselor or therapist) in constructively expressing anger directly to your ex-spouse, it is best that you express your anger elsewhere. This is a dangerous period for those unable to acknowledge their anger, because repressed feelings can explode into domestic violence.

The last phase of anger is forgiveness of both yourself and your ex-partner. Once the anger cycle has been fully experienced, it again becomes possible to communicate with your former partner in a calm and rational manner, and the need to get even and lay blame fades away under the force of forgiveness and the fact that you simply have better things to do with your life.

STAGE 2. LETTING GO OF THE EMOTIONAL CORPSE

(A) BURIAL

Normally, this is an easier phase for the dumpers who have already prepared for life beyond the relationship. It is difficult to let go of the past without some idea about where you wish to go in the future. The crab is reluctant to let go of its old shell until a new protective shell has begun to grow.

Letting go involves redirecting one's emotional investments from maintaining the relationship to maintaining oneself. Those who insist on "staying good friends" throughout the breakup are often avoiding the reality that the relationship has died and needs to be buried. Burials can be ceremonial; some clients report scouring the entire house to purge it of anything that reminds them of their ex-partners. Others have completely rearranged the furniture.

If you find yourself stuck in the letting-go stage, you might ask yourself what you are managing to avoid dealing with by not letting go. Parents who fail to let go often dwell for an overlong period either on all the good things or all the bad things about the other parent. The result is that the children will get caught in either the positive or the negative dealings between the parents, and that will prolong their adjustment process to the divorce. Plainly, letting go is a benefit to both parents and children.

The Psychological Divorce: Putting the Pieces Back Together

Evidence that you are letting go can be found when you think of your ex-partner only occasionally, when you rarely fantasize about being together again, when you stop trying to please him/her, when you rarely talk about the ex-partner with friends, when you stop generating excuses for face-to-face talk, and when you accept that there will be no getting back together.

(B) SELF-CONCEPT: MAYBE I'M NOT SO WORTHLESS AFTER ALL

Many spouses define themselves by their marriage and thus are devastated by the prospect of divorce. If the marriage is a failure then so, too, are they. Rebuilding your self-concept is a difficult and time-consuming task, but it is well worth the effort. In terms of phases, it begins with the simple yet profound decision to change oneself and one's perceptions. You can start on this simply by making a list of your good points as a human being. Like many others, you may spend hours on such a list and come up with only four or five good points, though you are able to write pages on your faults. This reflects low self-esteem; note that *the struggle to find positives is the first step to finding a new self-perception.*

Once positives are found and acknowledged, it is time to try to recognize some of the old patterns existing in the former relationship and to make sure they do not continue. Many of these old patterns can be compared to negative tapes in which you mercilessly blame yourself for everything that goes wrong in the world, while refusing credit for everything you have done right, calling these positives coincidences. Once such blaming cycles are recognized, it is possible to look beyond them, to change behavior and to feel a growing confidence in your new self.

As your new self begins to emerge it needs to be fed by new friends, new experiences, and generally positive interactions. This is a great time to give and get hugs. Working with a therapist at this point can be particularly beneficial.

Each child is also going through a self-concept cycle in which the child redefines what parents and family mean. The child's struggle should be recognized and supported.

Altogether, this can be a very exciting stage; after coming

through it, most people arrive at a point where they can feel good about themselves, their bodies, and their capacities as creative and autonomous adults to deal with whatever life throws at them.

(C) FRIENDSHIPS: THE FAMILIAR AND THE NEW

One of the most painful aspects of divorce is the loss of old and cherished friends. Women in particular report being deeply hurt when—as often happens—they are no longer invited to party with their married friends because some of the wives are suspicious of their single status. It is a sad fact that some friends cannot cope with the changes that occur in a person going through divorce. Still, while some friendships are lost, others are deepened; there is also great excitement in finding new friends who understand your emotional pain and do not reject you.

Getting to the point of establishing new friends, however, is not an easy task. Losing a number of your married friends can be a devastating blow to self-confidence, so many people find that their phones have begun to grow cobwebs before they are comfortable seeking out new friends. The first rule in seeking new friends is to seek *safe* friends. *It is too early to begin another intimate relationship.* Before you get together with someone, you need to get yourself together.

Interesting people can be met anywhere if you are interested in them. Clients have found new friends in grocery stores, hardware stores, at church, in community groups, while bowling, while running around the park, at lectures and concerts. The key at this stage is to find friends who are interested in you *as a friend* and not as a lover. Lovers will come and go and may take quite a bit of you with them. Your new self deserves a better and more stable support system of friends who can be relied upon. Working through this stage, clients are surprised to find that people actually enjoy being with them and that they have deepened their relationships with some of their old friends. There is no greater security than having close friends who know and understand you and all of your faults, and still care deeply for you.

The Psychological Divorce: Putting the Pieces Back Together

(D) LEFTOVERS: THEY'RE NOT ALL IN THE REFRIGERATOR!

Ending a relationship does not end the habits and problems that preceded it. Many people marry before they reach maturity. They simply move from obediently meeting their parents' expectations to obediently struggling to meet their spouse's expectations. Such people have never had or taken the opportunity to find out who they really are, and the fact of divorce forces them to confront leftover questions that should have been addressed years ago.

Leftovers have three phases: the shell phase, the rebel phase, and the love phase. The *shell phase* is completely "other-directed." The individual lives to please others as a means of avoiding the need to question himself. Crises occur when the wishes of a spouse and those of the parents conflict, and it becomes impossible to avoid displeasing someone.

The *rebel phase* occurs most clearly in teenagers who attempt to define themselves in opposition to authority. Among divorced persons, this attitude is embodied in the recently divorced male who becomes a sudden playboy with his sports car, flashy clothes, self-centered behavior, and new-found interest in significantly younger women. All of us want and need to rebel, but those who get through this phase most easily are those who try to *speak* and *feel* their rebellion rather than act it out. The first question is: Whom are you rebelling against? Your spouse? Your parents? Your brothers and sisters? Society in general? The next question is: What and whose expectations are you rebelling against? Are you a "rebel without a cause?"

The *love phase* begins once you are able to define yourself in your own terms rather than according to the expectations of others. At this stage you are better able to risk and learn from your mistakes while responsibly interacting with others. Now your choices are made on the basis of facts instead of the need to meet others' expectations or to maintain a wall of defiance and denial.

In sum, this is an exciting and essential period for both growth and prevention of a rebound relationship. Better relationships in the future depend on your having confronted your leftovers from past relationships. Clearly, this is a difficult task, but the effort is certainly worth making!

Leftovers also bother children because they have a limited number of behaviors with which to relate to adults. This is why many children relate to a stepparent in the same fashion in which they related to the original parent. The child may not change until he or she has worked through old emotions and learned new ways of relating.

(E) LOVE THYSELF AS THY NEIGHBOR

Some divorced people find it easy to love others and quite difficult to love themselves. They are basically "half-people" attempting to find wholeness through loving another. A love based on a fear-filled flight from emptiness and loneliness is unlikely to last. Realizing your self-love is basic to all productive, vital, growing relationships. Self-love means that you accept yourself for who you are. We must each appreciate and understand our strengths and our weaknesses.

Self-love does not mean that you love *only* yourself, but rather that your capacity to love and accept others is founded on your love and acceptance of yourself.

After a divorce, it's typical to feel that you have no capacity to love either yourself or others. This is a self-esteem issue, and there are many exercises to improve the situation. For example, you could list five adjectives that describe yourself, and then put a plus sign after each word that you think is positive and a minus sign after each negative. After you have done this, look at the negative adjectives and see if you can find anything positive about that particular aspect of your personality. The harder you work at this, the more positive things you're likely to find. Those who received scant love as children often have a great deal of difficulty loving themselves as adults. For some people, turning to (or returning to) their church, or a particular clergyperson, can be supportive and strengthening in this period.

Self-love is a particularly important issue for children involved in divorce. Many children feel that they have been shown to be unlovable, since one of their parents has left the home. They fear that the remaining parent will leave as well. This is a critical

The Psychological Divorce: Putting the Pieces Back Together

time for parents to do their best to reassure their children that they are cared for and deeply loved. This is very difficult for parents because children are often in need of the greatest love when their parents are least capable of providing it. Parents should make special efforts to explain to their children that, even though they are having doubts about themselves and each other as parents, they have no doubts about the love they feel for their children.

Those who have passed through the self-love trial often report that they emerge feeling securely lovable, and that they are no longer afraid of being loved or of loving another.

STAGE 3. RENEWAL

(A) TRUST: FOUNDATION FOR HEALTHY RELATIONSHIPS

Divorced persons are prone to complain that the opposite sex simply cannot be trusted or that "they are all turkeys." Pointing out such things is like pointing to a mirror: the mistrust reflects more of you than it does of them.

Trusting the opposite sex again is a difficult task, which must be accomplished cautiously. The key to this stage is to *make friends, not lovers*.

In many cases a divorced person plunges into a new romance before completing this stage, and the result is a relationship that is either dominating or desperate and often smothering. We must learn to trust before we can safely love.

Our incapacity to trust is largely a function of the wounds created by our divorce. Some who have been deeply wounded find themselves either avoiding relationships or indulging in brief, exploitative relationships where the other party has little or no power. Others feel that they must make every relationship into a lifelong love relationship. Trying to *make* a lifelong relationship often does nothing more than prolong the adjustment process.

Trust is a two-way street: trust in yourself allows trust in others. Trust demands openness and openness exposes you to the risk of disappointment or rejection. Start slowly and cautiously. Using caution, you can develop a healthier relationship style founded on your new sense of self-esteem. Clearly, the rewards are worth the risks.

Trust is an issue for the children of divorce. As we have emphasized, children will often blame themselves for one parent's leaving, unless the reason for the departure is clearly explained to them. The more trust you place in your children now, the more trust they are likely to place in you in the future.

(B) SEXUALITY: IT'S BEAUTIFUL!

Recently divorced people can be traumatized by the thought of dating. They feel they are old, unattractive, awkward, and that they no longer know the rules. To make it worse, they often have their parents' morality holding them back with the admonition to be "good." Furthermore, their own teenagers may be dictating their dating behavior by less-than-subtle suggestions. No wonder dating is confusing and uncertain and sexual hangups are so common.

Sexuality can be a major problem because it has been made such a big issue in this society. It is difficult to have a "normal" sexual relationship in a society where sex is used to sell everything from toothpaste to toenail clippers. Then, too, there is considerable confusion as to the role each gender should play, in this era of the sexual revolution. Can a man still pay the check without making the woman feel dependent? Can a woman call up a man and ask him out without seeming forward? These and many other questions make the resumption of sexual relationships both frightening and fascinating.

During the early stages of divorce recovery, it is common for the divorced person to be totally uninterested in sex. This is often followed by a period of deep longing for sexual contact that can be very difficult to deal with. Some cannot accept the idea of sex without marriage, while others are unable to accept their sexual feelings at all. One way to deal with this problem is to recognize that our bodies need to be touched and held, and that sexual contact is not necessarily the whole or the only answer to this need. Affection shown by and to friends and children can be a warming and reassuring way to maintain human contact until life can broaden out once more.

But as more personal—and potentially sexual—possibilities come into view, the key is to be both honest and cautious. Do not go beyond your comfort range, but do feel free to admit discomfort to your new social contacts. The fact that there are no clear rules for courting today can be frustrating, but it also provides you with the opportunity to set your own rules and create the best possible intimate relationship.

The sexuality stage is important for children because they need adult role models of both sexes. Children are often confused, frustrated, or intimidated by a parent's involvement in a new love relationship. Your attention is critical at this point, along with thoughtful and affectionate communication. You must make a clear, sincere effort to talk frankly about sex and relationships. Remember that your child's strong reaction may be less of a response to your new relationship, than to the fact that the child himself is just beginning to struggle with the whole notion of sexuality and independence.

Many people fail to progress beyond this stage, so it is very important to thoroughly deal with the issues raised here before proceeding to the next stage. You will have some indications that you have passed this stage when: you are comfortable going out with potential love partners; you know and can explain your present moral attitudes and values; you feel capable of having a deep and meaningful sexual relationship; your sexual behavior is consistent with your morality; and you are behaving morally, the way you would like your children to behave.

(C) RESPONSIBILITY: LET'S TREAT EACH OTHER AS ADULTS

This is a critical stage for learning from earlier relationships in order to improve future relationships. Many marriages that end in divorce are relationships in which responsibility has become unbalanced. Where the responsibility for support, affection, and decision making is not fully shared, the relationship is often not flexible enough to adjust to the stresses and changes in life. Accepting any rigidly defined role in your relationship can limit your capacity to grow within the relationship.

For example, some spouses fit into the roles of Prince and

Princess. The Prince/Princess relationship occurs where the Prince takes care of all of the Princess's needs and lives only to defend and shelter her from a difficult world. The Princess responds by worshiping him and becoming increasingly "helpless," in order to create opportunities for him to rescue/help her. Unfortunately, people good at helping are often poor at being helped, so the Princess becomes increasingly frustrated at being unable to serve her Prince. She feels he only needs her when she is helpless and needs to be rescued. She is frustrated by her increasing dependence. The Prince is frustrated by her attempts at independence.

The Prince/Princess phenomenon is alive and well today. Many of us have friends who took in stray pets while they were children, and seemed to continue the behavior as adults by taking on a "stray person" in marriage. *These people feel they are not lovable unless they are helping someone.* By marrying such a needy person, the Prince is minimizing the possibility of risk and rejection that is inherent in an *equal and dynamic* relationship.

"Givers" and "Princes" need to practice *asking for help*. This is done first with friends and then can be extended to lovers. It is just as important for you to share the troubles of *your* day, as it is for you to deal with the troubles of others. "Takers" and "Princesses" need to practice taking charge and helping. When you break out of your role you create flexibility within yourself and in your interaction with others. A relationship becomes stronger when both parties are able to help and be helped.

Passing this stage involves being able to identify which of your patterns are "over-responsible," which "under-responsible;" how they occurred in the past; and how they can be changed to create more flexible *adult* love relationships in the future.

(D) SINGLENESS: YOU MEAN IT'S OKAY?

Some people move directly from homes to the second home of college and then into the third home of marriage, without a period of time in which they are single and responsible for themselves. At this post-divorce singleness stage, emphasis should be on investment in your own personal growth rather than in other relationships. Such a period of singleness enables you to build confidence in yourself so that you can meet your needs and even enjoy singleness as an acceptable alternative lifestyle, instead of a state of utter loneliness. However, be alert to one common pitfall: Single parents often avoid new relationships by spending all their time at work or with the children and by being "too busy" for dates. This isolation can become a self-sprung trap that will make it much harder for you to go back out to meet the world as the new, whole individual you will have to be.

The point of working through the singleness stage is simply to become comfortable within yourself and by yourself. The goal is to be free to choose whether to remain single or to remarry. Granted, there is still a considerable amount of discrimination against single adults, but the situation has improved greatly in the past ten years. Dealing with discrimination against singles can often make you even stronger inside. You may find yourself calmly and firmly educating others about the realities of singleness, instead of walking away fuming from unkind, though innocent, remarks. This can be a peaceful and growing stage, as long as you do not use it to avoid all intimate relationships.

Lastly, your singleness is important for children because they need to learn to be independent from their parents in order to succeed in their relationships. Children who are able to see and understand the importance of living as single people are often better able to succeed in their own future love relationships.

(E) FREEDOM

Freedom in this sense is simply the freedom to be the person you were meant to be. This does not mean that your life will be blissful or that you will not run into any more problem relationships. Instead, it means that you have freed yourself from the expectations that have controlled you. The greatest enemies of divorce recovery are not the other spouse or the legal process; rather, they are the enemies that we all carry within us—such enemies as guilt, self-doubt, inadequacy, and fear of future relationships. When you achieve freedom, you no longer focus on the past. You are able to plan a future on your own terms and in your own direction, where you can express feelings of anger, grief, loneliness, rejection, and guilt, while actively pursuing a happy and self-fulfilling life.

Many clients report that periodic review of this chapter is helpful in providing a better understanding of the stages of divorce and a clearer understanding of their progress. Before going further into the divorce process, it is important to know your emotional needs.

CHAPTER THREE
DIVORCE MEDIATION: AN ALTERNATIVE

A BETTER IDEA?

IN DIVORCE, intense property, custody, and support disputes sometimes come from and express the ex-couple's underlying emotional conflicts. One premise of divorce mediation is that the anger, hurt, resentment, depression, and guilt a spouse carries from the marriage almost always needs to be addressed and handled carefully as part of a divorce. A second premise is that the adversary system, whether in court or in formal negotiations, may make a spouse feel less secure, more threatened, more depressed, and more hostile both in itself and by encouraging aggressive expression of each person's negative feelings.

To some extent we separate the psychological divorce discussed in Chapter Two from the litigated or negotiated property, custody, and support terms of divorce; leaving the divorcing spouse's emotional needs to his or her therapist, friends, or other resources. The importance of mediation is that it is an alternative process, in which the parties work together to resolve their emotional needs, during the same time that the financial and custody aspects of a divorce are decided. This chapter should help you decide whether divorce mediation would work for you.

Divorce mediation has come in for more attention nationally than it has in New York. California, for instance, has required mediation of child custody disputes since 1981. In New York there is pending legislation that may soon compel child custody mediation in all New York courts.

Mediation puts the mediator in the middle, as mediators deal with both spouses' needs and feelings, as they assist them to negotiate and to settle their disputes. A skilled divorce mediator is usually a matrimonial attorney or a trained therapist. The mediator will meet with both parties together and will encourage them to see the issues in terms of joint problems to be solved rather than as conflicts. For instance, a skilled mediator is likely to phrase the custody question as: "How can we insure that both of you will have the quality and amount of time with the children necessary for them to get full benefit from each of you as parents?" rather than as: "Who gets custody of the kids?"

The competent mediator, working with both spouses together, will encourage each to express any basic emotional issues that are standing in the way of ending the marriage, if it must be ended, with minimum damage. For instance, the wife may say that she can't trust anything her husband says about his business. She may, in fact, believe he would lie to defraud her of property; but perhaps what she really means is that she is so hurt by his betraying her and going off to live with another woman that she can no longer emotionally trust him about anything. In mediation, she may be able to first express and then to separate that pain from reasoned judgment; and, based on years of having shared everything with her husband regarding their finances, she may honestly conclude that he is very likely telling the truth about the money issues. One New York divorce mediator, attorney Lenard Marlow, says that in his experience with mediation, problems "dissolve" as their emotional underpinnings are dealt with.

PROBLEMS WITH MEDIATION

There are difficulties with mediation just as there are difficulties with what sometimes happens to divorcing couples who litigate. In particular, mediation is dangerous for a spouse who has been financially and emotionally subordinate during the marriage. Unless the mediator is very good, the agreement reached in mediation may be a continuation of the control or intimidation which the stronger spouse has previously exercised over the weaker.

Mediation also requires the voluntary participation of both spouses, and in many cases only one party wants the divorce. In our experience, it is wives who most often begin the legal divorce process, and they do so after a year or more of telling their husbands they want a divorce. The other spouse is often unwilling to participate in a mediation process leading to divorce, sometimes in hope that the mediation request is just more divorce talk that will go away if ignored.

Mediation does not remove your need to be advised by a competent lawyer, and your counsel should serve as a check against your signing an unwise agreement. Your lawyer should tell you whether the financial, custody, and support deal you are negotiating with your spouse is more, less, or about equal to what a judge would do for you after a divorce trial. A good lawyer can help you guard against one danger of mediation—that the informal, out-of-court procedures will miss or improperly value property that should be divided between the spouses. I suggest consulting with your attorney before and after each mediation session for input on the fairness and completeness of the agreements coming out of that particular session. Once the basic terms are settled, an attorney should write them into a separation agreement.

MEDIATION—ONE COUPLE'S EXPERIENCE

For over six months Betty had been dreaming of being alone, away. She wanted a divorce. But Betty was very mindful of the experience of her friends, Peter and Ann: they had just finished their divorce trial with experts and affidavits and "everything"—over $25,000 worth of everything. Ann won the custody battle, but neither really liked the decision. The money they had put aside for the twins' college had gone to legal fees. Peter was sliding at work, hitting the bars late, and hustling with a strange sort of blind fury almost any woman he could find. He had liberal visitation rights, but he hadn't seen the kids since the trial over two months earlier. Ann seemed mechanical and inaccessible. It appeared that there was just no way for her to get through her bitterness.

What had happened to their twins was the worst part of it. Sherry and Sheila used to be near the top of their class, but now they were slipping in school, and teachers reported they were "preoccupied," "listless," "apathetic," and starting to hang out with the "wrong crowd."

Betty felt there was no way she could put her family through that; yet she knew that Bob was very close to their children and might fight for custody, thus putting them through that kind of war.

She went to Sarah, a trusted lawyer friend, who told her about divorce mediation and mentioned the possibility of joint legal custody. Betty then told Bob that she had firmly decided on a divorce. Bob was angry and hurt and said "You can leave me but you can't take the kids." With Sarah's coaching and the help of a marriage counselor over the next several weeks, Betty was able to persuade Bob to begin mediation.

In mediation, Bob learned how to express his rage at Betty's wanting to end the marriage, and then was able to acknowledge that Betty's rejection of their life together did not mean she was less than a fine mother. The end result was an agreement leaving the children physically in Betty's home most of the time, with Bob paying child support, and giving both parents equal legal rights to make important decisions for the kids.

HOW IS IT DIFFERENT?

Mediation is often confused with conciliation and arbitration. There is considerable overlap in the techniques used for each process but, in general, proceeding from mediation to conciliation to arbitration involves giving an increasing amount of power to the neutral third party. Basic definitions are as follows:

Mediation: The process of bringing in a neutral third party to help two disputing parties come to a mutually agreeable settlement. The mediator does no individual counseling. The mediation role is limited to: (1) proposing basic ground rules for the parties' sessions to "keep them on task;" (2) helping the parties define or clarify the issues at hand, including emotional issues; (3) exploring alternative solutions so spouses can come up with a settlement best fitting their particular interests and circumstances.

Conciliation: The traditional distinction between conciliation and mediation is that the conciliator takes a more active role than the mediator in resolving the conflict, and perhaps in saving the marriage. Rather than simply being referees, conciliators may present their own solutions to a couple's problems. This distinction is sometimes blurred, however, because divorce mediators often use conciliation tactics in mediation.

Arbitration: Again, a neutral third party is used here, but the spouses agree to give the arbitrator the power to *decide the dispute,* as a private judge. In fact, some arbitrators are retired judges, and both sides are often represented by lawyers. In *binding arbitration,* the parties agree beforehand to abide by the decision of the arbitrator, as if it were law. The best source for traditional arbitrators is the American Arbitration Association, which is listed in your phone book.

Mediation is both a process and a product. As a process for parents, it forges a transition for the couple from a love/parenting relationship to a parenting relationship. The product of mediation should be more than the terms of a divorce: there should also be a mutually acceptable working agreement between parents who have gained from the mediation process an enhanced capacity to settle future disputes on their own.

Mediation keeps the power with the divorcing individuals. It provides an opportunity to structure parent-child relationships, to decide property questions, and to set support on the participants' terms instead of the lawyers' and the courts' terms. The feelings and principles of the people involved will form the basis for any mediated settlement. According to the late O. J. Coogler, one of the founders of modern family mediation, the "basic rule of structured mediation is that there should be no victims. . . . In court you don't know how it is going to come out. In most states, it depends on what judge you get that day, what mood he or she is in that day, and so on."

Coogler also believed that the participation and fairness of mediation prevents parties from being victimized. At a minimum, fairness means that family assets must be fairly distributed according to the needs and contributions of all and that children must have access to both parents.

Naturally, each side's concept of fairness can change during mediation. According to John Haynes, a former associate of O.J. Coogler, "That's the magic of mediation." Mediation should hold a mirror up to each party so that he or she can better see the impact of his or her demands and better understand the needs of the other.

Sometimes hard feelings between parties prevent the compromise necessary for negotiation. Mediation can provide a forum where these feelings are aired. Court rarely does so. It is common to go to court to vent anger or vindicate one's position. When both sides present limited and unrealistic views of their family situation, the judge, despite his or her best efforts, can be forced into making a limited or "winner-take-all" decision. Courts must make their decisions on the evidence before them, and that evidence is subject to strict rules that drastically limit testimony.

Mediators can help their clients to deal with anger, fear, and other feelings so that these do not block the progress of settlement. Mediation demands that spouses communicate honestly with one another in a structured setting where they are encouraged to clearly state their principles and positions and to negotiate in good faith. This can be difficult at first. Some spouses are flatly unwilling to mediate, or are incapable of doing so. An exercise to determine your willingness and capacity to mediate is presented later in this chapter.

MEDIATION—HOW IS IT DONE?

The actual techniques of mediation differ with each practitioner and family. According to John Haynes, "One part of mediation is to lay out all the options. I look at every problem in divorce as a skein of wool that has to be carded. We have to look at each problem—children, finances, the family home—one by one. Then I will try to separate out each problem into component parts. Then I look at all the options I can think of and ask the parents to think of options of their own. . . . Perhaps it's the way we were educated, but most people come in with this idea that there is really just one way to do things; that there's just one way to think about dividing up the children's time, for instance, when there are perhaps five or six ways, or more, and we can begin to explore all the options before making any decisions."

With rare exceptions, mediation of custody disputes is *future oriented*. The past cannot be changed. The task is to determine how, starting right *now,* the parties can become cooperative, responsible, and separate parents.

There are a number of mediation procedures. For illustrative purposes, O.J. Coogler's *Structured Family Mediation Method* will be summarized. "Structured Family Mediation" uses one mediator, who is not an attorney, plus an advisory attorney who is brought in later in the process to answer deferred legal questions and draft the Settlement Agreement. Mediation by two mediators (one a family law attorney, and the other a trained therapist) is also possible, and may be more effective in dealing with difficult cases. Under Coogler's system, mediation sessions take place once a week and last two hours each.

THE PROCESS

ORIENTATION SESSION

Here the terms and conditions of mediation are explained and, if the parties wish to proceed, an agreement is signed, and an advance deposit for ten hours of mediation is paid. Coogler has six basic rules for mediation:

1. The mediator cares about both parties and their children but will not represent any side.
2. The participation of both parties in mediation is voluntary, but the mediator will not allow either side to coerce, abuse, or lay blame in an effort to force the other to agree to take any particular action.
3. Everything that occurs in mediation is confidential and should not be used in court if mediation does not succeed.
4. Any agreement the couple comes up with must be based upon adequate information, which means that both sides must agree to fully disclose what they know about family finances.
5. The mediator cannot require the mother and father to cooperate, but he or she can keep them from negotiating with one another in noncooperative ways. In other words, minimum civility is required during these sessions.
6. The mediator will not endorse any agreement regarding the custody of a child that does not provide for contact with both parents.

SESSION I

Hour 1: The first issue to be faced is the agenda—deciding the order in which issues will be considered. The parties are free to set any order they prefer. A common agenda is as follows:

1. Custody arrangements
2. Identification and division of marital property
3. Spousal maintenance (if any)
4. Child support
5. Child custody and visitation

Next, the participants will provide information on their finances and financial needs and the session will be concluded with the drafting of a temporary Settlement Agreement. The *purpose of a temporary Settlement Agreement is to maintain the status quo* during mediation and does not compromise either party as regards the final decision.

Hour 2: If there is no custody controversy, the parties should agree on visitation. The children can be present in this session, but this often requires an extra session. After visitation, marital property is considered. First, the property is fully disclosed, then valued, which, for property of a complex nature or uncertain value, may necessitate bringing in experts. Couples rarely bring full property information to the first session, so even a tentative division is deferred.

Once the combined budgets of the parties are provided, the mediator checks to see if the total exceeds their combined income. If it does, the parties are directed to look separately for ways to reduce their budgets or increase their incomes.

SESSIONS II AND III

Hours 3–6: Here the participants work to flesh out the specifics of property division, support, custody, and visitation. Anyone needing more time can request it and prepay the fees to cover the anticipated costs. Extra time allows the mediator to suspend discussion on any issue (custody, for example) on which the parties are deadlocked, and to return to it later after other issues have been resolved.

SESSION IV

Hour 7: If the parties are in agreement on all the basic issues, an advisory attorney is brought in to examine the settlement and to answer any deferred legal questions. Answers to legal questions often require further information from the clients, so more time may be scheduled here.

Hour 8: If the legal questions are fully answered during the preceding hour, the advisory attorney will at this time present his/her previously drafted proposed Separation Agreement for examination. Further time can be scheduled, if substantial changes in the agreement are needed, or if the parties wish to consult their own attorneys.

Session V

Hours 9–10: If custody is still unresolved by this time, then all financial issues that can be resolved without considering custody should be put in a written agreement, leaving custody and visitation for the end of the last session. Before the custody discussion opens, there should be agreement as to whether or not the children will participate. The degree of participation by the children must also be previously agreed upon and made clear to the children during the session.

If there are further difficulties, parents should be reminded that no custody arrangements are permanent and that they might wish to opt for a temporary arrangement, after which time they can decide to (a) continue the arrangement; (b) agree to change it; or (c) agree to return to mediation if they don't agree on the changes necessary.

There are many other methods of mediation with different degrees of structure. All methods encourage the parties to proceed as they see fit.

MEDIATION—IS IT FOR YOU?

On the basis of what you have read so far, you may now be able to make some decision about your readiness for mediation. Readiness depends first upon willingness and next upon capacity. Dr. Sheila Kessler, a prominent trainer of mediators, offers the following checklists to help determine how you stand in relation to mediation.

MEDIATION: HOW TO FIND YOUR MEDIATOR

There are many divorce mediators and mediation groups in New York State. Some divorce mediators are attorneys experienced in family law; others are professionals trained in mental health. Your acquaintances in either group may be able to refer you to a good mediator. Also you may contact the Divorce Mediation Council of New York State, 200 Garden City Plaza, Garden City, New York 11530, (516) 294-5848, for a reference.

Divorce Mediation: An Alternative

AM I WILLING TO MEDIATE?		
1. Is each issue (for example, custody of our children) negotiable?	Yes ___	No ___
2. Am I willing to make some compromises?	Yes ___	No ___
3. Do I trust my former spouse enough to think he or she will uphold a mutually satisfactory agreement regarding the children? (There is almost always some doubt.)	Yes ___	No ___
4. Am I willing to deal with my anger for a while so that I can confront the issues in a rational manner?	Yes ___	No ___
5. Can I truly live up to what I agree to (regarding the children)?	Yes ___	No ___
6. Am I capable of listening to the other person's side of the story?	Yes ___	No ___
7. Do I see this process in terms of compromise rather than of winning or losing?	Yes ___	No ___

If your answers are mostly yes to these questions, you are probably a good candidate for mediation. The next checklist will help you determine if you are ready. You should be able to answer most of the following questions. Do not be discouraged if you cannot provide detailed answers to the questions right now. Think of answering this checklist as an initial assignment.

Our recommendation is that you pick a mediator with thorough knowledge of the New York divorce laws, whether or not he or she is an attorney, and also consult with your own attorney between mediation sessions. We have all had husbands come in after long mediation processes, which they thought were successful, though they had been guided by inexperienced mediators. Each thought he needed only a simple legal drafting up of the mediated agreement. Their wives also consulted attorneys,

---

AM I READY TO MEDIATE?

1. Do I know what my current income is and what I can anticipate in the future? Yes ____ No ____

2. Do I know what my former spouse's income is and what he or she can anticipate in the future? Yes ____ No ____

3. Do I know what the household budget was before I separated? Yes ____ No ____

4. Have I drawn up a reasonable budget for my household, if a shared parenting plan is worked out? Yes ____ No ____

5. Have I drawn up a reasonable budget for the parent with the *majority* of child-rearing responsibilities, if a shared custody plan is not worked out? Yes ____ No ____

6. Have I drawn up a reasonable budget for the parent with the *minority* of child-rearing responsibilities, if a shared custody plan is not worked out? Yes ____ No ____

7. Have I calculated the financial assets from the marriage (the value of the house, cars, investments, furniture, pension plans, etc.)? Yes ____ No ____

8. Have I thought through how I would like the day-to-day parenting arrangements for my children to be set up for the next couple of months? For the next year or two? Until the children are of age? Yes ____ No ____

and in each case the wife's attorney informed her that the mediated agreement was not complete and was not fair to her in terms of what a judge would likely do after a contested trial. The mediated settlements came unraveled, and we've had some angry husbands as clients. The results probably would have been better, if each mediator had known enough to advise the parties fully, as mediation proceeded, on what their legal rights were, or if the parties had each consulted his or her own attorney during the mediation process, instead of first making a deal and then checking.

Individual mediators' experience, competence, and techniques vary markedly, and we believe it is best to get a referral from someone you trust and go with that mediator, if the first mediation session seems right. Some couples may wish to interview several prospective mediators before they choose one; but the choice often gives the couple something else to disagree about.

CONCLUSION

Divorce mediation has both significant promise and significant problems. For the right couple, it can reduce the potential harm of litigation, increase communication skills, decrease the trauma to the children, and increase the value and strength of the family that will come out of a divorce over what it would otherwise be.

CHAPTER FOUR

CHOOSING YOUR LAWYER

A DECISION to divorce is usually painfully difficult. Once it is made, you are faced with another decision: How do you find a lawyer who is right for you? That decision is necessarily intertwined with another judgment you must make: Do you want to try for a mediated or negotiated settlement without going to court? If you believe that you and your spouse are capable of negotiating a settlement either directly between yourselves or through your attorneys, then your attorney should have negotiating skills and the knowledge of New York divorce law and federal tax law needed to draft a technically good separation agreement. The lawyer's litigation experience and ability are less important to you. However, if you believe that a war will be necessary to get satisfactory results with your spouse, or if your spouse has already hired a bomber as his or her attorney, then you may need a good courtroom lawyer to effectively protect your interests.

A PERSONAL DECISION

Before you select a lawyer you must assess your expectations of the attorney-client relationship. After all, you are buying into a highly personal, although temporary, partnership where mutual confidence is a key consideration. This relationship is highly individualized, so it is worth looking around before deciding upon the attorney you will hire. Some lawyers can at once make a client feel secure and comfortable. Others may not be as personable, but may be extremely imaginative in looking for solutions to your particular problems.

Do you expect the attorney to help you decide whether to divorce, or to act as a marriage counselor? If so, you are probably making a mistake. Most lawyers are not qualified to aid you in this way, unless they also are trained as marital therapists. Lawyers tend to be concerned primarily with getting the legal process started, documenting your financial situation, readying forms for filing, and developing effective strategies. These are the tasks they have been trained to do.

You may also wish to consider mediation, which is described in the preceding chapter, and you may want to defer starting the formal legal process while you try mediation. You will need an attorney who is available for legal advice while you are in the mediation process and who can draft a technically sound separation agreement after you and your spouse settle the basic property, support, and custody issues in mediation.

Look for a lawyer whose practice is principally involved with marital dissolution work. A lawyer's fine reputation in immigration law, for example, is largely irrelevant to your needs. Ask if your potential attorney has been an active member of family law committees in local, state, or national bar associations, or is a member of the American Academy of Matrimonial Lawyers, a group that admits only attorneys primarily doing family law. Also make certain your divorce lawyer has experience with the courts and the legal community of your area. But your own gut reaction, after you have gathered the necessary facts about the lawyer, is your most important guide in finding the right attorney for you.

THE ADVERSARY SYSTEM

This discussion of choosing an attorney, whose training and experience typically include both adversary negotiations and court trials, seems the right place to summarize our misgivings about divorce litigation. You may wish to raise these questions with your own prospective attorney and get his or her views on the costs and advantages of various approaches to ending your marriage.

This book leans against full-scale litigation and courtroom trials as a way of settling matrimonial disputes. Divorce proceedings with two hard-nosed attorneys facing each other in court or in no-holds-barred negotiating sessions may solve the legal and economic aspects of divorce, while harming the social and psychological aspects, which are just as important. Dr. Max Cohen, a psychiatrist who does divorce mediation in New York, says the adversary system in divorce is perfect for very sick people. The litigation process encourages each divorcing spouse to use tools that will inflict severe pain on the other spouse, destroy whatever trust and goodwill are left in their relationship, and invite equal or greater pain as the other spouse retaliates.

The adversary process itself may leave each spouse embittered, even though a full-scale trial never occurs; preparing for a fault divorce trial is traumatic, as each spouse dredges up and relives those of the other party's bad acts which are relevant to trial. One woman I know described the effects of preparing for trial against her husband as "ripples." She said that five years after her case had settled just before the trial was to begin, those ripples were still doing damage, not only to herself and to her children, but also to her friends and to her work. Such ripples from bitter divorces have contributed to adjustment problems in children, which show themselves in school performance, drug use, early pregnancies, and other problems. Prolonged stress from the process can even harm the divorcing spouse's own physical health.

A real cost of litigation is that divorce terms that are imposed by a court are much less likely to be complied with than settlements to which both parties agree. A judge can issue a piece of paper called a divorce judgment which imposes rights and obligations on the divorcing spouses, but the judge is not there to implement his orders. An aggrieved ex-wife or ex-husband can keep running back to court for orders enforcing the divorce judgment, but the process is expensive and in many ways unsatisfying.

PROBLEMS WITH DIVORCE LAWYERS

A very fine judge was recently the third speaker at a seminar for lawyers about the New York divorce law. The first two speakers had described with skill and clarity the complex, formal procedures the divorce lawyer can use to identify and to value a couple's marital property. The judge began, "When I heard the previous speakers say it takes two years to get a divorce case ready for trial, I say what about the clients?" He continued that a system that accepted leaving people in limbo for two years, neither really married nor divorced, might need to be replaced.

The lawyer is trained as an advocate, not a problem-solver. The adversary system of justice encourages and even demands that the attorney use every legal means available to gain an edge for his or her client. The essential problem—legally ending a dead marriage quickly, efficiently, and fairly with minimum damage to the spouses and to their children—is often forgotten as the spouses fight and watch their lawyers fight.

The work in a contested divorce is often a challenging and fascinating game—for the lawyers. We can use our lawyer skills to analyze and to communicate interesting legal concepts, to make strategy, to out-maneuver the opposing attorney. The game rewards intellect, imagination, and nerve. As lawyers, we can measure our success by a bottom line at the end of the game: How much property, custody, or support did the client get or not give up? That score, however, ignores the pain endured, opportunities lost, and the relationship problems which the adversary process may have created, as far as the client is concerned.

YOUR ATTORNEY FEES

Legal fees can be a problem in litigation or extended negotiations. Even with the best and most ethical attorney representing you, divorce litigation is expensive. It is time-consuming, and the lawyer is selling you his or her time. And, to be blunt, there are New York divorce attorneys who will intentionally make your divorce litigation longer and more complicated in order to increase their own fees. One judge, who had sat for a year exclusively in the matrimonial part in New York County, spoke of his experience there with an attorney who had been hired to represent the wife in a "large asset" case, after another attorney had represented her in two years of negotiations and litigation. At a conference in court, the judge thought that all the roadblocks to a settlement had been removed. The new attorney, however, said "Judge, the case isn't ready to settle." The judge reviewed the issues that were solved and his view that the case was already settled. The new attorney had to repeat twice more "Judge, the case isn't ready to settle" before the judge understood that the attorney was not *willing* to let the case settle because he had not had enough time to build up legal fees.

Anger at an attorney and at legal fees is often, however, a client's way of venting anger at the fact of a divorce he or she does not want, or at other history not related to the lawyer. The client may lack the courage or self-awareness to take responsibility for the marriage's failure, and be tempted to make the lawyer, as a participant in an unwelcome process, the whipping boy.

Louise Raggio (Grier Raggio's mother and a Dallas attorney who has been helping people through divorces for thirty years) once represented a woman client of unusual self-insight and candor on this matter. The divorce had been concluded on favorable terms for the woman, yet she still objected to paying reasonable legal fees and was extremely upset. In conversation, she told Louise "It hurts too much to be angry at my former husband and my children, and I have to blame someone, so I am taking my anger out on you."

Whatever your legal fees, we will give you odds that the

money you pay your lawyer will not be the greatest cost of full-out adversary litigation. To avoid a matrimonial war, it may be helpful to come from the point of view that you, as well as your spouse, are responsible for the breakdown of the marriage. If you are able to see yourself as responsible, you are well on your way to avoiding the "prove I'm right, prove he/she's wrong" scenario characteristic of litigation. Ideally, both spouses and their attorneys will see the death of the marriage as creating a set of financial, legal, psychological, and social problems that they will work together to solve. In doing so, they will create an appropriate post-marriage relationship that will support the couple's needs and the needs of their children.

REPUTATION AND RECOMMENDATIONS: KEY QUESTIONS

Most people choose lawyers through their reputations or by asking for recommendations from persons whose opinions they value. Divorced friends are a good source of information, particularly if their cases were satisfactorily resolved. Use caution, however, and evaluate your friend's lavish praise (or angry denunciation, for that matter). Inquire closely about those qualities that your friend either admired or disliked in the attorney. You may want to ask some of the following questions:

- Did the attorney's efforts interfere with or facilitate your friend's relationship with the former spouse and their children?
- Did your friend feel personally secure and comfortable with the attorney?
- Did your friend come away from the process feeling informed?
- Did your friend feel that the attorney's fees and the results of the divorce trial or settlement were fair?

If you follow this route, be sure you see the lawyer to whom you were referred, not his or her associate or partner. Remember that you may want to interview several lawyers until you find the one who suits you. This is your right. You are the employer, and in such a critical matter as divorce it is essential that you find an attorney with whom you can communicate and in whom you can place your trust.

For personal referrals you may also turn to various organizations, your employer, or your labor union. In New York City, the Association of the Bar of the City of New York at 36 West 44th Street, (212) 382-6625, will, through its Legal Referral Service, refer you to a lawyer selected as suited for your case. Many other counties have Lawyer Referral Services; their addresses and phone numbers are listed in Appendix E. The New York State Bar Association has a statewide Lawyer Referral Service in Albany, which New York residents may reach through an in-state toll-free number: 800-342-366l. Under their LRS plan, a lawyer will consult with you for half an hour without charge or for a prescribed low fee, usually $25 in cities. The LRS fee is $15 for the first half-hour in 37 more rural counties. If your income is low, you may qualify for free legal services through a legal aid program.

If you are referred to a lawyer who is a stranger to you, you can sometimes get background information about the lawyer by consulting the *Martindale-Hubbell Law Directory* in the public library. This Directory includes a roster of most members of the bar in the United States and Canada and some other foreign countries. Listings paid for by the lawyer or the lawyer's firm appear in the Directory's Biographical Section and include the lawyer's biography and educational background. The biographical listing frequently includes those areas of practice that the lawyer or firm emphasizes.

LEGAL CLINICS: THE PROS AND THE CONS

An alternate method of employing a lawyer may be to take advantage of one of the "legal clinics" that have appeared recently around the country and in your phone book's yellow pages. These clinics often handle uncontested divorces at low rates. They are able to charge less because they work on a large volume basis and use simple, standardized forms, with extensive help from paralegal assistants. The clinic uses a factory approach which is fine if only a small amount of property has accumulated during your marriage and there are no serious support or custody issues. Depending upon where you live, an uncontested divorce might cost anywhere from $150 to $500, not counting filing fees. Fees charged by legal clinics are usually set in advance and are based on a published schedule. Lawyers are available during the day, in the evening, and on Saturdays; also, credit cards are accepted, and the initial consultation is often free.

Remember that not all divorce cases lend themselves to the clinic approach; standardized procedures will not work for complex cases. A law clinic is simply a high-volume, high-efficiency law firm. Since the cost per case is low, the firm can afford to set low fees. High volume, however, carries its own risks. There probably will not be the expertise needed for complex cases. Clinics are rarely appropriate for cases that involve problems with property division or child custody.

THE INITIAL CONFERENCE: A CHECKLIST

During the initial conference you should ask the lawyer questions, as well as give information. You need information to determine whether this attorney should handle your case. Your basic standard for choosing will be your own gut reaction to the lawyer personally and as a professional, but answers to the following questions may assist you in formulating or reinforcing that reaction.

1. What are his or her credentials?
   (a) Having attended a well-known law school is no guarantee of outstanding ability; however, it helps to know the lawyer's academic background.
   (b) Does the lawyer belong to the city or county bar association? This may indicate respect among peers and suggest respect among the local judges.
   (c) You can check to see on which sections or committees of the bar association the lawyer has served. If he or she has

served on sections or committees related to family law, such as the family law section or the taxation section, or if the lawyer is a member of the American Academy of Matrimonial Lawyers, chances are you're dealing with one of the more committed lawyers in your areas.
  (d) Look around the office: you'll see the degrees, diplomas, professional memberships, and honors the lawyer has attained. Perhaps you will not even need to ask about credentials.
2. What portion of the lawyer's time is spent in family law matters? Many lawyers, particularly in New York City, now deal almost exclusively in divorce cases.
3. What is the lawyer's attitude toward arbitration and mediation? Many lawyers agree that the adversary process is inappropriate to divorce cases and are willing to explore alternative forums to resolve disputes between couples. However, some are not so inclined. If yours is a case that you feel can be resolved without a courtroom confrontation, and this lawyer believes that "the truth" can only be found in the adversarial process, then you had better look elsewhere.
4. Is the lawyer willing to discuss the attitudes of local judges concerning issues relevant to your case? Many lawyers are able to predict accurately in most cases what the general outcome of a trial would be, based on the prevailing judicial attitudes. Getting the client to accept those predictions is often the hardest part of our job. This would be a good time to discuss specific strategies for your case.
5. What is the lawyer's attitude about joint legal or physical custody? In the recent past, most lawyers and judges discouraged even the thought of this kind of arrangement. Now that joint custody concepts have gained wider acceptance, there are more enlightened lawyers who, in suitable cases, will consider this as an alternative to the traditional custodial arrangement.

YOU ARE THE EMPLOYER: A CLIENT'S BILL OF RIGHTS

It is important to let your lawyer know exactly what quality and type of legal service you expect. According to some studies, there are "enormous differences between the client's view of what was wanted from legal services and the lawyer's view of what the client wanted." (Morgan, *Client and Public Relations, A Lawyer's Handbook,* Revised Edition [1975].)

Although lawyers often assume that the result is the main criterion used by clients in evaluating their services, other less tangible factors are often more important to the client. One survey concluded that clients respond more favorably to friendliness, promptness, and lack of condescension, and value being kept informed by their lawyers.

You can control your own divorce proceedings by paying attention to the following, which we call the "Client's Bill of Rights" (and responsibilities):

1. Find out your lawyer's qualifications and experience in family law matters at the first consultation.
2. Insist on a written retainer agreement that explicitly sets out the lawyer's responsibilities and the lawyer's fee structure.
3. Stay informed about the progress of your case by requesting copies of all letters and documents prepared or received in the lawyer's office in your behalf. Ask questions: communication is a two-way street.
4. Determine early how the lawyer plans to represent you and what course of action is expected to be taken during the divorce process.
5. Be aware that you can always change lawyers even if you have signed an agreement. As long as you have paid to the point at which you part, the lawyer cannot prevent you from taking your file with you should you decide to change lawyers.

Again, the relationship between client and lawyer is that of employer and employee. You are the employer, and you have an absolute right to fire your employee at any time, even without cause. Note, however, that when you change lawyers you will duplicate some of your expenses up to that date because your new attorney will have to become familiar with the facts of your case, and you will likely have to pay for the time this will take.

Conversely, there are a number of responsibilities you as a client should observe if the lawyer is to be as effective and as efficient an advocate on your behalf as he or she can be:

1. Use a checklist (like the one provided in Appendix B) when you first consult the lawyer so that a quick profile can be established regarding your case. Include with the checklist relevant documents identifying and valuing your property. This can save your lawyer hours of work and can mean lower fees.
2. Do not expect your lawyer to guarantee results. Although the lawyer can, and probably will, make predictions about the outcome of your case, the actual outcome of negotiations or litigation may turn on very complex factors.
3. Always keep your lawyer informed of any new developments that might affect your case.
4. Take your lawyer's advice, or get another lawyer. You are wasting your money and the lawyer's time if you do not have confidence in the lawyer's special knowledge and skills.
5. Be utterly candid with your lawyer; tell the truth. Legal advice is worthless, if it is based on faulty or partial information. Tell your lawyer every fact that is relevant to the situation, being careful to include all facts that do *not* appear to be in your favor. Lawyers can plan effective strategies around adverse facts, but only if they are aware of them.
6. Avoid phoning your lawyer repeatedly about petty matters. If you write down your concerns in the form of a letter, you might be surprised to see how many of these matters are not consequential. You may decide not to mail the letter. Remember that the lawyer has other clients who also require attention.

THE ATTORNEY'S ETHICS

You should expect and demand from your lawyer nothing short of utmost zeal, confidence in you, and honesty. Once retained by you, the lawyer is obligated, both by law and by the lawyer's own ethical code, to be completely loyal to you. The lawyer should permit neither personal interests, interests of other clients, nor the wishes of third persons to diminish total commitment to you. This includes a commitment to accept employment only for matters in which he or she is competent. If the lawyer does not have the expertise to handle your particular divorce case, he/she should refer you to an attorney who does.

If you become dissatisfied with your lawyer and decide to use another, you should be aware that New York permits the original lawyer to assert a "lien" against whatever paperwork you have already provided in connection with your case. If the papers are originals that you need for your divorce or other matters, the lawyer has great leverage against you, until you have paid the fee. Your new lawyer can help you negotiate this matter.

If you believe your lawyer overcharged you, acted unethically, or has failed to represent you fully, report this to the disciplinary committee or grievance committee responsible for the lawyers in your county. These committees operate under the supervision of our appellate judges for disciplining unethical lawyers. For more information, contact the bar association in your county or speak to a clerk in your county's courthouse. Appendix F is a list of New York State's Supreme Courts by county, with addresses and phone numbers.

CHAPTER FIVE

THE BASICS OF NEGOTIATIONS

BARGAINING IN THE SHADOW OF THE LAW

YOU HAVE decided to divorce, have chosen a lawyer, and have gathered necessary information on the family's economic situation. What happens now? Usually, negotiations. This is not a totally new skill you have to learn. We negotiate every day. Those who have children know that a normal three-year-old is an instinctive negotiator for the important things in life: staying up another ten minutes, not eating the carrots until you promise candy, and so forth. We each bargain and attempt to persuade in just about every aspect of our relationships with other people, and we do so when we divorce.

In divorce, what do you negotiate? Potentially everything. Who pays whom and how much? Who gets the house? Who gets custody of the children and who pays for college?

Except for those who ignore or boycott the divorce process (or feel priced out of that market), the economic, custody, and support issues in nine out of ten dead marriages in New York are eventually settled by a private bargain between the divorcing spouses rather than by a judge's decision, after a full-scale trial in court. Settlement is highly probable unless one or both parties persist in being unreasonable, spiteful, or determined to prove that he or she alone is "right."

The negotiations leading to agreement may take a week, they may take two years, or even more. The process may be businesslike and polite; equally it may be noisy, bitter, and interrupted by frequent trips to court. The husband and wife may do much of the bargaining directly, using their lawyers as advisers and draftsmen, or they may leave all the face-to-face negotiating to the attorneys. They may use a mediator to assist them in their own direct negotiations, as described in Chapter Three. The bargaining may be completed before a lawsuit for divorce is even started; sometimes the parties do not settle until they are in the middle of a contested trial after years of fighting. But the odds are that your case will in some way, at some time, be settled by you and your spouse, rather than by a judge after a trial.

Many divorce judges, before and even during a trial, strongly encourage the couple to reach their own settlement and thus conserve court time. The judges recognize that the lawyers, who may have represented the parties for two years or more before trial, know much more about their clients, the clients' needs, and their resources than a judge will learn in a trial. A settlement drafted by the lawyers is therefore more likely to maximize total benefits than is a judge's decision.

In this chapter you will find basic information about negotiation techniques and strategy in divorce cases. A college classmate of ours, Robert H. Mnookin, is co-author of an excellent Yale Law Journal article titled "Bargaining in the Shadow of the Law: The Case of Divorce." That title concisely states what a divorce case is often about, particularly where there is substantial property to be divided.

Divorce negotiations are "in the shadow of the law" in the sense that they are partially shaped by the parties' estimates of what a court will do if no agreement is reached and the case goes to trial. For instance, until 1980 the New York divorce law provided that a wife ordinarily had the right to receive alimony from her husband after a divorce, but that no court could order an ex-wife to pay alimony to her ex-husband, except in a case where he was about to go on welfare. The divorcing husband, therefore, had a very weak bargaining position when he asked his wife for financial help, even if she was rich and he had difficulty supporting himself. If she refused, the New York courts could not help him, since the law could not require a woman to pay alimony to a man.

Under present New York law, the court can require either spouse to pay "maintenance" (the substitute for what used to be called alimony) to the other, depending on the facts of the case. That gives the husband who has difficulty supporting himself more bargaining muscle. If his financially stronger wife refuses his request for support, he can force the case to trial and the judge will have power to order her to pay him maintenance.

So as we negotiate, we look over our shoulder at what the court will do about property, maintenance, child support, and custody, if you and your spouse do not reach a negotiated settlement. Obviously, you need information about what a court would likely do if there were a contested trial. Your lawyer is your obvious source for those predictions. Most of the rest of this book focuses on giving you a general knowledge of the legal principles that New York courts use in deciding divorce cases and that your lawyer uses in predicting outcomes. That knowledge will empower you to participate more fully and more creatively with your attorney in negotiations. This chapter focuses on conventional adversary negotiations rather than the softer, problem-solving type negotiations, emphasizing the parties' emotional needs discussed in the chapter on mediation. The theory and technique of your own negotiations will probably be a blend of the two. Further, purer forms of both types of negotiations may be appropriate at different stages of the same case.

YOUR JOB

You have already listed the property you and your spouse have accumulated, itemized your income and expenses, and gathered other facts your lawyer requested. Now think of what you *most* want in a negotiated divorce settlement. Your initial answer on maintenance and child support and property may be "as much as I can get" or "as little as I can give," depending on your situation. Or it may be "I just want a fair result that ends the marriage and allows me to get on with my life quickly."

Perhaps you can be more specific. If it is already agreed that you are to have custody of the children, sole ownership of the house may be very important to you and for your (and the children's) emotional and financial security. You may need a high income for a few years until you complete your work for a graduate or professional degree. You may have a business that you want to protect from your spouse. Your most important need may be quite narrow: I once represented a woman whose first priority was protecting her job with a large company which her husband's friends owned and her husband operated. She had worked there for many years, and her job gave her much personal satisfaction. Her age and background made it very difficult to move to as good a job with another employer, so she wanted to stay in her position even though her ex-husband would be her boss. We negotiated a deal which made it risky for her ex-husband to have her fired.

Look at your emotional attitudes toward the divorce and toward a negotiated settlement. Clients are prone to say things like: "If you don't see that Jim is a horrible person, you aren't on my side." You may believe that your spouse is a miserable so-and-so, and by some objective criteria that may even be true. But if you feel you should use the divorce proceeding to punish your spouse for all the bad things he or she has done to you, our strong recommendation is that you look at the costs of doing so, which we have outlined in earlier chapters. Further, you need a clear head to pursue your own best interests effectively.

YOUR ATTORNEY'S JOB

Your attorney should know New York divorce law, his/her way around in divorce courts, and the facts of your case. Using this knowledge, he or she may predict for you what a court is likely to do after a trial. These predictions are often very difficult to make early in the case for several reasons. Firstly, the equitable distribution statute was passed by the New York legislature only in 1980, and it is still uncertain how the courts will interpret and apply many of its provisions. Secondly, the statute is complicated and gives the trial judge enormous discretion and flexibility in applying the law to the facts of an individual case. Thirdly, your attorney may need time for a detailed investigation to gather important facts about your spouse's property and income, or about how best to structure the custodial and visitation arrangements.

If you are doing your own negotiating, you need whatever predictions your attorney can give you before getting into the custodial or financial aspects of your divorce with your spouse. You should also get his or her advice on negotiating strategy and tactics. If your attorney is doing the negotiating, you should discuss what you *most* want in a settlement, given the attorney's evaluation of what negotiating leverage you have. Whoever bargains, both you and your spouse should be clear on what your negotiating objectives and priorities are before starting the process.

YOU AS A NEGOTIATOR

In our experience, strong, rational client involvement in the negotiating process usually leads to better agreements because the client's preferences are more fully incorporated in the deal. You know what your needs are better than your attorney does. It's your life, and you should participate in the choices necessary in dividing property, setting maintenance and child support, and in all other aspects of terminating the economic partnership that is part of your marriage.

We sometimes encourage our clients to negotiate the basic terms of divorce settlements directly with their spouses. This works best where there is approximate equality between husband and wife in bargaining ability and both want to reach an agreement. Many of our clients, particularly women, come to us wanting a champion and protector and do not feel inclined or equipped to directly participate in negotiations. We, of course, respect their wishes and do the negotiating personally, with frequent consultations with the client. Even when appropriate, direct participation in negotiations does *not* mean that the client writes the agreement or negotiates all the details. The settlement agreement, particularly where large amounts of property have accumulated during the marriage, will be a complicated, technical document which will require good legal drafting. The husband and wife often can define the broad outlines of settlement for themselves—who gets custody, who gets the house, how much maintenance and child support. After each discussion the couple has, we confer with our client to evaluate whether the tentative results of the negotiations are reasonable and to suggest additional issues that need to be resolved.

ANALYZING YOUR SPOUSE

You and your lawyer have discussed your wants and needs, the strengths and weaknesses of your case, and you are emotionally able to move toward a negotiated settlement. Now you should *listen* carefully as your spouse communicates his or her needs, and analyze what you have that your spouse most wants. The idea is to give the other party something you have that is very important to him or her, but less important to you. In return, you get something that is more important to you than it is to your spouse. Let us illustrate with a hypothetical case, where ongoing negotiations cost unnecessary time and pain:

John and Ann's marriage was clearly over by the time John moved out of their house and went to live with his girlfriend. Ann sued for a divorce, then refused to go ahead unless John gave her more money than he felt he could pay. New York is among a backward minority of states where divorce still requires "fault" such as adultery, abandonment, or cruelty by one of the parties, unless the parties reach an agreement. The vast majority of states bury a dead marriage at the unilateral request of one spouse who alleges "breakdown of the marriage," "incompatibility," or a similar no-fault ground.

Ann used New York's fault law as a negotiating tool and dropped her divorce suit after a year, even though the marriage was clearly over. She thought John's impatience for a divorce meant that she could get more money negotiating with him than a court would give her after a trial. John knew he could not get a fault divorce against Ann if she contested his lawsuit. Ann had good negotiating leverage; John wanted a divorce badly while Ann did not mind staying legally married, so long as she did not have to live with John. She used that leverage openly, telling him "You can have your divorce anytime you want," if he first met her financial demands.

WHAT DOES HE/SHE WANT?

Ann's cards were good, but she overplayed the hand and failed to make a quick deal. After two years of stalemate, John was very frustrated at the law's failure to solve his problem and remained unwilling to give Ann as much money as she wanted. John considered moving to another state to get a no-fault divorce there, but decided against it. He then tried another approach, which was to give Ann what she didn't want—namely, John at home. He walked into the house and said, "Sweetie, you're right. We're married and I'm home." Ann left unhappily when John insisted on staying in the marital home that night and the following nights. His actions led to a property settlement after a few weeks and then to a divorce.

This illustrates several points. There was a good negotiating opportunity, which was lost shortly after John left the house. Ann had something, the power to give John a divorce, which was very valuable to John and which had little or no value in itself to Ann. It was reasonable for John to pay Ann something extra for a quick divorce, and he was initially willing to do so. A settlement would have allowed both parties to get on with their lives and avoid the stress on themselves and their children, which years of uncertainty and legal fighting always produce. The settlement opportunity passed, and John then forced the issue by doing something he found unpleasant, but which was even more unpleasant for Ann: returning home.

REMEMBER LONG-TERM COSTS AND BENEFITS

Again, keep in mind that, where there are children, an ex-couple will continue to be involved with each other even after divorce. Support, custody, and visitation are ongoing processes, and negotiation or litigation tactics that leave one party or the other bitter may turn out to be quite expensive. If you both focus on giving your ex-partner what is comparatively more valuable to him or her and taking back what is comparatively more valuable to you, the chances are high that you will quickly reach an agreement and move on with your lives. But it takes two sides to negotiate, just as it takes two to fight. You should not allow yourself to be bullied or threatened as you negotiate your divorce agreement. If the other party tries to get an unfair agreement by intimidating you, you need to show firmness. Perhaps your resoluteness, and your attorney's, will change your spouse's attitude over time. In the meanwhile, patience—and going to court for whatever temporary protections you need—is the proper strategy.

It is also wise not to box yourself in with ultimatums or written-in-stone positions. Have a clear idea of *your* interests and be creative and flexible in negotiating to advance those interests. Negotiation becomes difficult when the parties think in terms of absolutes and dictate terms that they become glued to.

RISK-TAKING

Part of bargaining "in the shadow of the law" is knowing that, if you and your spouse do not reach an agreement, a court is available to impose its solution on both of you. To illustrate some principles of risk-taking in negotiations, here are some examples that ignore both the uncertainties usually present in real divorce cases and the noneconomic costs of matrimonial litigation we have discussed.

Imagine that you and your spouse have $100,000 to divide between you. Imagine further that if you cannot agree on how to divide the $100,000, the two of you will together spend $20,000 of the $100,000 in lawyers' fees before a judge decides the case.

Finally, imagine that both you and your spouse know that the judge probably would divide the remaining $80,000 evenly between you, so that after a trial you would each have $40,000.

If you conclude that the judge would divide the $80,000 evenly, why not agree between yourselves to divide the $100,000 equally, thus saving the $20,000 in lawyers' fees and other costs? You may do so, but it is quite rational for you to push for close to $60,000 of the $100,000. This is because your spouse knows that if there is no agreement and the case is litigated, he/she will get only $40,000; thus any settlement that gives him or her more than $40,000 is an economic improvement over the probable result after litigation. There is a $20,000 range in which both parties will get more by settlement than by litigation; dividing that $20,000 may require some pushing and shoving between the two of you. If one party insists on $55,000 and will not be moved, the other has the choice of taking $45,000 in a settlement or litigating and getting $40,000. The first spouse runs risks in demanding $55,000; the second may choose to give up $5,000 and litigate, perhaps even out of a spiteful desire to cost the first spouse the $15,000 difference between the $55,000 settlement demand and the $40,000 litigation result.

THE COIN FLIP

Your tolerance for uncertainty and risk may affect your success in negotiating such problems. Imagine that you had the choice between a sure $50 and a coin flip which would decide whether you took $100 or nothing. If you have a strong desire to choose the coin flip over the certain $50, you are a risk-preferer in the situation. If you have a strong preference for taking the sure $50, you can be said to be risk-averse. The risk-preferer has an advantage over the risk-averse spouse in negotiations—for example, the dividing up of the $100,000 discussed above—for he or she has a greater tolerance for the possibility of losing. The risk-averse spouse may take the $45,000, particularly if he/she is convinced that the other party is comfortable with the risk that a deadlock will leave each with $40,000. The risk-preferer will, other things being equal, be more inclined to push for the lion's share of the $20,000 at the risk of losing half of it. The risk-averse party will tend to settle for less than $50,000.

Whether you are risk-averse or a risk-preferer may depend not only on your psychological makeup, but also on your economic ability to tolerate the prospective loss. Herb Cohen in his book *You Can Negotiate Anything* illustrates the point. He frequently asks his audience how many would accept a bet where Cohen would pay $1,000,000 if a coin toss came up heads and the audience member would pay Cohen $100,000 if it were tails. Very few people offer to take the bet because very few people can afford to lose $100,000 at the toss of a coin, even if winning means $1,000,000. Cohen states that many would accept if the bet were $100 against $1,000 because most of us can afford to lose $100, and 10-to-1 are good odds. Risk-aversion may greatly diminish negotiating strength if the other side knows and chooses to exploit that aversion to risk.

TRIALS ARE ALWAYS RISKY

The inherent uncertainty in the judicial process gives the risk-preferer spouse an advantage over the risk-averse spouse. Your lawyer will give you his or her best estimates of what is likely to happen at trial, but New York courts have enormous discretion in divorce cases and the judge's decision may be quite different from your lawyer's prediction, for better or for worse. You can avoid that uncertainty by reaching agreement now, but a relatively small tolerance for uncertainty may leave you needing an agreement more than your spouse does. One of the basic rules of commercial negotiations is that to make a good deal, you should seem prepared to walk away without a deal. If your spouse knows that you cannot stand uncertainty and risk, he or she may insist on unfair concessions before giving you the certainty you want, by signing a divorce settlement.

Finally, it is a cliché that a good settlement is one that completely satisfies neither party but with which each can live. If your side wins too much and the opposition gets too little, the whole agreement is more apt to come unhinged, and costly litigation may ensue. Where both sides feel that the terms are fair and reasonable and were arrived at by give-and-take, there is psychological and moral pressure to abide by the agreement, in much the same way you are honor-bound when you "shake on it." Studies have shown that, where the parties arrive at support terms by negotiation and agreements, which are found by the court to be acceptable, the obligor pays, and pays on time, more frequently than when support terms are imposed on the obligor by a court. This word to the wise should be sufficient: avoid arrearage and enforcement problems if you can.

CHAPTER SIX

PROPERTY DIVISION

ON JULY 19, 1980, the Equitable Distribution Law became effective in New York State and the rules for divorcing spouses shifted massively. The law is still fairly new as statutes go, and many important questions about how it should be interpreted and applied have not yet been answered by our courts. We state what we believe the rules are or will be, based on existing New York court decisions and on the experience of other states with older and more settled marital property laws. Some knowledge of the pre-1980 rules may help you understand the present rules, and also why your friend's 1979 divorce terms are not a very useful guide for current divorces.

THE OLD ORDER

Before the 1980 law became effective, marital property was only property that was titled in both names, such as a marital home owned "by the entireties" or a joint savings or bank account with "rights of survivorship." The old laws gave New York judges few powers to divide property between divorcing spouses. Imagine, for instance, that a husband had started and built up a restaurant chain during a twenty-year marriage while his wife stayed home with the children. The business was a corporation, and he owned all the stock. On divorce, the wife had no claim to that property because title to the stock was not in her name. She could ask the court for alimony, and the court was required to order the husband to pay based on her needs and his ability to pay, but she was deprived of a share of the property accumulated during the marriage. The situation was even more unfair if the husband had little income and the accumulated property was in the wife's name, for New York courts also had no power to order a wife to pay her husband alimony.

The old title system was inadequate, and many New York attorneys, including the authors of this book's Introduction and Appendix A, worked for years for laws giving divorcing New York spouses property rights similar to those long enjoyed by citizens of "community property" and "equitable distribution" states. On alimony, the United States Supreme Court ruled in 1979 that statutes giving women, but not men, rights to seek alimony were unconstitutional, and so New York's old alimony statute became unenforceable.

THE REVOLUTION

Overnight, with the passage of the Equitable Distribution Law, New York's marital property law became one of the most sophisticated and progressive in the country. The statute enumerates ten factors which New York courts are to consider in distributing "marital property" and ten factors to be used in deciding whether and how much "maintenance" is to be awarded to a spouse. The essential property concept is that marriage is an economic partnership, and that the property accumulated during a marriage is to be divided equitably on divorce, regardless of which spouse holds legal title. Men have gained equal rights with women to seek alimony, now called maintenance.

Appendix B contains the text of the Equitable Distribution Law; we suggest that you read it, if you expect to be closely involved in negotiating property division or maintenance issues, and refer to it again, as need arises. Our explanation of the concepts and implications of marital property, separate property, maintenance, and other terms used in the statute will be more meaningful to you if you read the law itself. Again, we return to our friends Mary Ellen and Jim for illustration of the principles involved.

CONTINUING SAGA

Mary Ellen returned to our office shortly after Jim moved out. She brought to this meeting the checklist discussed in Appendix C. The task of accounting for her monthly expenses was proving to be difficult. It was hard to focus on utility bills, insurance premiums, taxes, and the like. She wished she had been more familiar with those figures during her marriage. We had to assure her that, although this exercise was difficult, it was essential. She said,

> "Each time I sit down to attack those financial forms you gave me, my mind blurs. I just can't keep my thoughts straight. Then when I got to the questions about our insurance and Jim's pension plan, I knew I didn't have a clue! I felt so helpless. Jim and I plan to get together so he can help me list *our* assets.
> "It's so mechanical and stark putting dollar values on sixteen years together, and dividing everything up. It's hard for me to do that when I'm still feeling so emotional."

We gave Mary Ellen information on the emotional stages of divorce (see Chapter Two, "Psychological Divorce") to show that her feelings were not unusual. Nevertheless, she was told, our first priority was to assess the property to be divided. Until this was accomplished, we would be without a clear picture of her future resources.

In New York, *The premise of the New York marital property and alimony (now maintenance) laws is that modern marriage should be viewed as a form of economic, as well as social partnership.* Therefore, all remaining assets acquired during the marriage by individual or joint efforts or expenditures should be equitably divided upon dissolution. It is the product of the marital partners' economic efforts that constitutes the kitty for equitable distribution. We assured her, however, that property division did not occur in a vacuum. Many factors are considered, including the future earning power of each spouse.

Mary Ellen was convinced she could never find a job that would pay enough to allow her to adequately support herself and two teenagers. She loved her home and her neighborhood. Would this divorce cause her to lose her present lifestyle?

We emphasized again that this is why the division of property is one of the most critical aspects in the divorcing process. Two households are about to be created out of a single household, and in most families this demands changes in the living standards of both parents and their children. Mary Ellen wanted the house and some income-producing property to supplement the maintenance and child support she expected from Jim. She knew that owning property would make her feel more secure after the divorce.

DIVIDING MARITAL PROPERTY

Except in cases involving marriages of short duration, no children, and limited marital property, the task of property division is not easy, technically or emotionally. The current Equitable Distribution Law and the presence of tax problems require detailed accounting of the marital assets. The cold mathematical facts of property settlement often do not fit well with the emotional aspects of divorce.

Courts go through a four-step process to reach a full and fair division of the total assets, and individuals in negotiating or in mediating property division should go through a similar process. By completing a questionnaire we gave her, Mary Ellen and Jim got started on the first steps in the process, which are:

1. Determine which property is "marital" under the statute and which property belongs solely to one party, making it separate, or non-marital, property.

2. Value each significant item of property.
3. Consider how debts, attorney fees, and other closing-down expenses should be provided from the economic resources at hand.
4. In light of all of the above, and by applying the factors enumerated in the Equitable Distribution Law, the court will decide how to divide the marital assets most equitably. Sometimes an equitable result can be best achieved by providing for a "distributive award," requiring monthly or periodic payments from one spouse to the other, rather than by dividing a chunk of marital property. Under New York law, *equitable does not mean equal;* it means fair, in view of all the circumstances.

MARITAL PROPERTY OR SEPARATE PROPERTY?

In New York courts, only marital property will be equitably divided between the spouses upon divorce. The separate property, as statutorily defined, of each party will generally remain that party's alone.

Generally speaking, *separate (or nonmarital) property* consists of all property acquired before the marriage and all property acquired after marriage by gift (except from the spouse), by inheritance, or as compensation for personal injuries. Separate property also usually includes property acquired in exchange for other separate property and the increase in value of separate property (unless the nonowner spouse has contributed to the appreciation).

Marital property generally consists of *all* nonseparate property acquired during the marriage, unless there is a valid agreement between the spouses that provides otherwise. This includes all purchases made with the earnings of either or both, regardless of who holds legal title to the property. For instance, if the wife starts a real estate brokerage during the marriage, that business will be marital property, even though her husband does not have title to any stock in the business, and even though only the wife's earnings went into starting the business.

New York courts view the marriage as a partnership, so that

any assets accumulated during the marriage are presumed to be marital property. Therefore, those accumulations produced by individual or joint efforts or expenditures should be shared equitably, upon the termination of that relationship by divorce or annulment. Separate property remains with the owner-spouse, though the court may allow the spouse with custody of the children to occupy the marital home during the children's minority even though that home is technically the separate property of the other spouse.

Property acquired after the parties sign a separation agreement or after one of the parties starts a matrimonial lawsuit, but before their marriage is dissolved, is generally regarded as the separate property of the spouse who acquired it. The rationale is that the spouses are no longer working together in the interest of the marriage partnership.

YOU CAN DECIDE

Spouses, however, are legally authorized to determine the character, or definition, of their assets for themselves. That is, they may agree on what is marital property and what is separate property, and the courts will honor that agreement even though it gives a result that differs from what a judge would decide in a trial under the Equitable Distribution Law. *To make these personal agreements enforceable, they must be in writing and signed by the parties with all the formalities required for a deed.* The agreement will be enforced by the divorce court, whether it was entered into before or after the parties married, as long as it was "fair and reasonable" when made and "not unconscionable" at the time the court divorces the parties.

By such agreements, spouses can also change the status of their property at any time. For example, a husband may wish to make a gift of the family home to his wife. Courts generally uphold a couple's rights to contract with one another to make marital property into separate property; but when the spouses later divorce, the courts will take a very close look to make sure that the former marital property is now truly separate. Usually, the burden of proof will be on the spouse who at the time of divorce is displeased with the definition of the property. He or she may argue that the transfer was part of a larger estate plan, or was made for protection against creditors. In the absence of agreement otherwise, the statute says that gifts between spouses are marital property.

Mary Ellen, for example, always wore one truly lovely diamond ring. The ring had been left to Jim upon his grandmother's death. Mary Ellen had enjoyed wearing it for the ten years preceding the breakup. Did this ring constitute Jim's separate property? Possibly—unless Jim had given it to her at the right time and in the right way. If Jim had given the ring to Mary Ellen before they married, it would be her separate property. If he gave it to her after they married, it would be marital property, because gifts from one spouse to the other are marital property *unless there is a formal written agreement* otherwise.

SEPARATE PROPERTY IMPROVEMENTS AND INCOME

As a general rule, any income or increases in value attributable to separate property during marriage remain the separate property of the owner-spouse. However, some recent cases have ruled that even if separate property increases in value during marriage because of the owner-spouse's *active* management, the increase in value becomes marital property. Income from separate property, and the property itself, may be considered in determining a fair and equitable division of all property. For instance, if the court realizes one spouse will be receiving monthly income from a separate property trust fund and the other spouse has no separate property, it will tend to award the second spouse a larger portion of the marital property than it otherwise would. If one spouse directly contributes to an increase in value of the other spouse's separate property, then the appreciation due to the nonowner spouse's efforts or expenditures clearly becomes marital property. Examples might be the husband who served as the unpaid carpenter for renovation of a building his wife had purchased before the marriage, or the wife who served as the unpaid decorator on a home owned by her husband. Moreover, some New York decisions hold that spousal contributions in general, such as keeping the home and raising the couple's children, may qualify a spouse for a share of the appreciation of the other's separate property.

VALUING YOUR PROPERTY

Every item of property has its value. Spousal agreement as to the value of property can be a difficult but not insurmountable task. Just as one person's junk is another's antique, certain items of personal property may have a very high value to one spouse.

On the birth of their first child, Jim gave Mary Ellen a solitaire diamond, which cost $3,000. He thought that the diamond was probably worth at least $4,000 today; for sentimental reasons, Mary Ellen felt it to be beyond price. Imagine their surprise when the gemologist put its market value at $2,500. Mary Ellen held that the ring should not even be considered part of their property settlement—after all, it had been a gift from Jim. Negotiations almost broke down when Jim insisted it be valued and put into the marital property kitty. Eventually Mary Ellen "bought" the diamond from Jim at market value by giving him an offset against other marital property.

Often divorcing couples let sentiment cloud their judgment when valuing their assets. Each views their accumulations, whether a residence or a birdcage, as somehow intrinsically part of himself and therefore not to be parted with, except at great price to the other spouse. Louise Raggio tells the story of a $5 million settlement that was collapsing because both spouses insisted on having the one chain saw in their garage. Louise went out to a hardware store and bought a second identical chain saw. The parties laughed at themselves and then signed the agreement. I have seen carefully drafted, complex million-dollar settlements evaporate over the disputed value of a dining table or a set of encyclopedias. To paraphrase the poet Robert Burns, would that we could see ourselves as others see us—when we wrangle over the birdcage.

MINIMIZING THE VALUATION DIFFICULTY

To the extent that he/she can, each individual should sit down and rationally set market values on all the marital personal property (furniture, appliances, jewelry, etc.). If their figures do not agree, each should state the value to himself or herself of the item. The high bidder can then take the item from the marital property pot at the high bid price, resulting in a credit to the other spouse at that value. Imagine the husband's shocked expression when, after he has self-servingly stated a $10,000 value on household furnishings actually worth $4,000, the wife responds "Alright, I'll take the cash, you keep the furniture." It's surprising how close this bidding process comes to setting a true market value on these personal items.

Once sentiment is removed from the process of valuation, the couple should be able to determine a reasonable value for most of their personal property. In valuing furniture and other household items, they should be guided, not by what they paid for the item, but by what it would sell for in the marketplace. (Some call this "garage sale" value, especially when it applies to used furniture.)

Market value is technically defined as the amount of money that a buyer (who is willing but not obligated to buy) would pay an owner (who is willing but not obligated to sell) for a particular piece of property. Market value is *not* the amount of money required to replace the item, nor is it what the item might bring at a distress or liquidation sale.

Costly or rare items of property, like the residence, acreage, expensive jewelry, antiques, and paintings, will probably require the services of an appraiser for proper valuation. Even then, a mathematically precise valuation is impossible because appraisers (like lawyers and spouses) can honestly disagree. Nonetheless, the court will require present values based on the realities of the market place. The owner may give the court his or her opinion on an item's value. But the professional appraiser's opinion, supported with facts, figures, and particularly information on recent sales of comparable properties, will probably carry more weight with the court.

SPECIAL CONSIDERATIONS AFFECTING VALUE: TAXES, SALES COSTS

For many items of property, particularly realty, the cost of selling the property should be considered when fixing its net value. If, for example, a home is to be sold, the net equity will be reduced by the broker's commission, attorneys' fees, and other closing costs.

The court may also consider reducing the market value of an item by the amount of taxes that might be incurred upon a subsequent sale. An example would be two shares of a corporation's stock, one purchased early in the marriage at a lower price, the other purchased later on in the marriage at a higher price. If Mary Ellen took the share purchased at the lower price and then she and Jim each sold, Mary Ellen would net less than Jim, even though they sold at the same time and at the same market price, assuming their marginal tax rates were equal. This is because the capital gains tax on Mary Ellen's sale would be greater than the tax on Jim's sale, since she had a lower tax basis on her stock than Jim had on his. *Taxes affect the sale of most items.* If the tax consequences are substantial enough the court may be persuaded to consider them when setting a value on the item. *The federal Tax Reform Acts of 1984 & 1986 substantially affect persons considering divorce.* See your tax attorney or accountant for specific information.

IF YOU CAN'T AGREE, THE COURT WILL DECIDE

If the spouses, either directly or through their attorneys, cannot agree on the division of their marital assets, the court will complete the task, guided by the legal principles of equity and fairness contained in the Equitable Distribution Law. This does not necessarily mean there will be an equal division of the assets. As we have said, equality is not always equity. The Equitable Distribution Law provides that the court, in granting a divorce, must distribute the marital property between the spouses, and that it shall do so "considering the circumstances of the case and of the respective parties," as well as the statutory guidelines.

THE BIG 13 OF MARITAL PROPERTY DISTRIBUTION

The 13 factors listed in the marital property distribution portion of the Equitable Distribution law must be weighed and balanced by a judge when he or she divides and distributes marital property after a divorce trial. Each of the 13 factors may have more or less value or weight, depending upon the case's overall circumstances. We will therefore briefly discuss each of the 13 factors a court is *required* by the law to consider in distributing marital property.

(1) *the income and property of each party at the time of marriage, and at the time of the commencement of the action*

The divorce court has power to distribute only marital property; it must leave separate property with the spouse who has it. But factor (1) permits the court to give the spouse who has less separate property a greater share of the marital property. Imagine that a husband inherited a fortune during the marriage and the parties accumulated a much smaller sum as marital property during marriage. A court, using factor (1), would tend to give most of the marital property to the wife because she has less separate property.

(2) *the duration of the marriage and the age and health of both parties*

Where only one spouse earned significant income during the marriage while the other, typically the wife, stayed home with the couple's children, the court will tend to increase the wife's share according to the length of the marriage. In a long marriage, say twenty years or more, where the wife has devoted herself to the home and to supporting the husband's business activities, factor (2) would influence the court toward giving more of the accumulated marital property to the wife. Similarly, if the wife is relatively old for the job market or in poor health and so less able to become economically self-supporting, the court will tend to give her more marital property.

(3) *the need of a custodial parent to occupy or own the marital residence and to use or own its household effects*

If the wife has primary custody of minor children, the court will tend to give her possession and occupancy, and in some cases ownership, of the spouse's marital home. This is for the benefit of the children as well as their mother, as it may lessen the traumatic dislocations and uncertainties that divorce brings for children. Of course, if the father gets custody, the court will want to give him possession and occupancy of the house. Where the house is jointly owned, the court may order it sold when the children reach majority and the net proceeds to be divided.

(4) *the loss of inheritance and pension rights upon dissolution of the marriage as of the date of dissolution*

During marriage, each spouse has the right to take part of the other's estate on death, regardless of what the deceased spouse's will provides. Similarly, many pension plans give important rights to a surviving spouse. These contingent economic benefits are lost upon divorce. Therefore the court will lean toward giving more marital property to the poorer spouse and the one with smaller accumulated pension benefits.

(5) *any award of maintenance under sub-division six of this part*

If one spouse is paying maintenance (alimony) to the other, the recipient has less need for income from property. Conversely, the spouse paying maintenance may need more property to generate the income needed to pay the maintenance, so the statute instructs the court to consider maintenance and marital property division together, in an attempt to reach an overall economic result that is just.

Property Division

(6) *any equitable claim to, interest in, or direct or indirect contribution made to the acquisition of such marital property by the party not having title, including joint efforts or expenditures and contributions and services as a spouse, parent, wage earner and homemaker, and to the career or career potential of the other party*

Factor (6) is the key issue in many equitable distribution cases. Assume that the wife worked while the husband earned his M.B.A. She then stayed at home with the children while he built his own consulting business and accumulated investment properties, title to which was taken in his name alone. Assume further that the wife frequently acted as the unpaid bookkeeper, office manager, and hostess for the husband's business associates. At divorce, it is fair for the court to lean the wife's way in passing out the stocks, bonds, land, and so forth that the husband's business has generated. The husband will keep getting income from his skills and his personal business contacts after the divorce, but the wife can get a return on her "investment" in his education, skills, and business contacts only through maintenance or through getting a bigger share of the distributable marital property.

(7) *the liquid or nonliquid character of all marital property*

The husband may have built up a profitable business during the marriage with assets that cannot be sold quickly for their full value, or, for instance, there might be corporate stock that is restricted and cannot be sold publicly until years after it was issued. The court may give full value to those assets, leave them with the owner-spouse, and compensate the other spouse either with more easily transferable marital property or with a "distributive award."

The drafters of the Equitable Distribution Law created an innovative and flexible distributive award device. A court can balance its grant to a husband of a business considered marital property with an order that the husband pay a certain sum of money, either all at once or in installments, to the wife at or after the divorce, to compensate for her not being granted any portion of the business. Those payments are intended by the law to be part of, to supplement, or to substitute for the distribution of marital property, and, therefore, not to be taxable income to the wife, as maintenance payments would be.

(8) *the probable future financial circumstances of each party*

If the wife has devoted herself to the home and to furthering the husband's career instead of developing her own earning potential, it makes sense to give her more of the marital property. She will have more difficulty accumulating new property than the husband will. On the other hand, if one spouse has a large amount of separate property, from inheritance or whatever source, that guarantees his or her future financial security, the court may tend to give the poorer spouse more of the accumulated marital property.

(9) *the impossibility or difficulty of evaluating any component asset or any interest in a business, corporation or profession, and the economic desirability of retaining such asset or interest intact and free from any claim or interference by the other party*

In the consulting business case used in discussing factor (6), the husband's M.B.A., skills, and personal business contacts are important assets because they greatly increase his earning power. But they cannot be transferred to the wife or to any third party who might want to buy them, and thus do not have an exchange value. The business may have goodwill value because the husband has been consulting for years and has a large number of customers who keep coming back to him and referring others. But that goodwill may not be fully transferable because the customers are personally loyal to the husband.

The court cannot transfer any portion of the husband's education, skills, or business contacts to the wife. Nor would it be sensible for the court to require the husband to sell his business, even if it could be sold, and divide the proceeds, since the wife's and the children's future support may depend on the husband's ability to earn income from his business. What the court can do is give the wife an extra share of other marital property or a distributive award as discussed in factor (7).

(10) *the tax consequences to each party*

This factor (10) was added by the 1986 amendment, although previously it was considered under former catch-all factor (10). The amendment simply makes tax consequences an *express* statutory factor. One party may have a higher marginal tax rate after the divorce than the other, and both parties may come off better in an arrangement in which taxable income is shifted to the spouse with the lower tax rate. For instance, where there are two pieces of property each worth $10,000, but one property has a tax basis of $2,000 and the other has a tax basis of $7,000, it makes sense to give the first to the spouse who will likely have the lower tax rate when the assets are sold. In that way the overall taxes are cut down. However, the spouse taking the asset with the higher tax liability should expect to be compensated elsewhere in the economic divorce package.

(11) *the wasteful dissipation of assets by either spouse*

This factor was also added by the 1986 amendment to the Equitable Distribution Law and merely expresses in statutory form the holdings of prior cases. Note, however, that the word "assets" is not qualified by a term such as "family" or "marital" and may include *separate assets*, if broadly construed. In any event, an extravagant wife or a gambler husband may be penalized by the application of this factor.

(12) *any transfer or encumbrance made in contemplation of a matrimonial action without fair consideration*

Again, the 1986 amendment merely expresses the prior New York decisions and holdings on this issue. For example, a husband may not strip himself of assets by giving them to a lover or relative, in order to make a smaller property distribution, or in the hope of reducing maintenance.

(13) *any other factor which the court shall expressly find to be just and proper.*

This is former catch-all factor (10) which has been renumbered (13) and is intended to cover situations not covered by the other enumerated factors.

DIVIDING THE INDIVISIBLE: SPECIAL ASSETS

By their nature, some assets are not easily divisible. If the court must award a specific asset to one of the spouses, provisions are made to compensate the other. What cannot be divided can often be traded.

The jointly owned family residence is usually an indivisible asset. Most courts will award possession and occupancy of the family home to the spouse having custody of the children. This is done partly in an attempt to minimize further disruption of the children's lives. Therefore, if there is no additional property of equal value to effect a trade-off with the noncustodial spouse, the custodial spouse may receive exclusive possession of the home for a number of years, on the understanding that the residence will then be sold and the net proceeds of the sale be divided equally between the spouses. In the meantime, the noncustodial spouse might be given a compensating lien against the residence. The divorce judgment often provides that the home will be sold, should the custodial parent remarry, enter a cohabitation relationship, no longer use the home as his or her primary residence, or die, whichever occurs first.

Pensions and retirement benefits may be forms of deferred compensation, in which there is a spousal interest which should be valued in the event of divorce. Moreover, pensions are the largest marital assets for many divorcing couples. An actuary will often be necessary to determine the value of each specific plan. Pensions or other entitlements of employment will often be allocated to the employee spouse, while other marital property is given as a set-off to the nonemployee spouse. Or the court may require that pension benefits be divided "if, as, and when" received by the employee spouse. If the pension rights are not to be divided as received in the future, then the court will determine the present value of the pension rights and factor it into the marital property distribution.

BUSINESS GOODWILL

Goodwill is property of an intangible nature, and it is often relevant for divorcing professionals. The accountant, dentist, eye doctor, lawyer, or whatever, by virtue of training and past performance, may have established a professional practice that promises a good future income. The nonprofessional spouse has been a silent partner in building the practice and is now forced to withdraw from the partnership. The valuing of a goodwill invariably requires the services of an expert, usually an accountant, an economist, or a business broker experienced in selling professional practices. A business such as Jim's medical equipment corporation may also have goodwill that an appraiser will consider in appraising its value.

PROFESSIONAL LICENSES: O'BRIEN v. O'BRIEN

If one spouse becomes a doctor during the marriage, is the professional license marital property? New York's highest court said "yes" in the case of *O'Brien v. O'Brien,* published in December 1985. Most other states say "no," often on the grounds that a professional degree or license is not property, since it cannot be transferred from the license holder to another person. The legal principles that New York's Court of Appeals announced in *O'Brien* apply to licenses to practice law, accounting, dentistry, and other professions. We will review briefly the facts in Dr. and Mrs. O'Brien's marriage as an aid to applying those legal principles to other situations.

The trial court found that nearly all of the O'Briens' nine-year marriage was devoted to the husband's obtaining a license to practice medicine. When the two married, they were both teachers. Shortly after the marriage, the husband returned to college to complete his bachelor's degree and sufficient premedical courses to enter medical school. The couple then moved to Mexico for three and one half years, during which the husband attended medical school and the wife worked to pay the couple's expenses. They then returned to New York, where the wife resumed her teaching career and the husband completed the school and internship work necessary for his license to practice medicine. Two months after Dr. O'Brien got that license, he started a divorce suit against Mrs. O'Brien. At trial, Mrs. O'Brien claimed that the license was marital property and that she should receive part of its value. The Court of Appeals agreed.

The *O'Brien* decision noted that New York's Equitable Distribution Law is premised on the idea that a marriage is, among other things, "an economic partnership," and said: *"As this case demonstrates, few undertakings during a marriage better qualify as the type of joint effort that the statute's economic partnership theory is intended to address than contributions toward one spouse's acquisition of a professional license."*

HOW DO WE VALUE A PROFESSIONAL LICENSE?

Once it was decided that the license was marital property, the next question was how to value it. The Court of Appeals held that a professional license's value "is the enhanced earning capacity it affords the holder." At trial, an expert for Mrs. O'Brien had testified that Dr. O'Brien's license was worth $472,000, that being the present value of the higher earnings the expert estimated Dr. O'Brien would enjoy because of his having medical training and his license. The trial court ordered Dr. O'Brien to pay Mrs. O'Brien 40 percent of that value, or $188,000, in eleven annual installments. Since the O'Briens had no children and Mrs. O'Brien was capable of supporting herself by her teaching, there was no child support or maintenance to be paid from Dr. O'Brien's future earnings.

The *O'Brien* concept that a professional license acquired by one spouse during marriage is marital property, and that its value can be divided between the spouses by a divorce court, will enormously complicate the valuation and division of marital property for many couples. What should a court do if one spouse earned a professional degree early in the marriage and each spouse has enjoyed the professional's higher earnings and property accumulations for twenty years before divorce? How does a court avoid double-counting, that is, requiring the professional spouse to pay the other a portion of the present value of the license and also requiring higher maintenance and child support because of the professional's higher future earning ability? Courts have much discretion under the Equitable Distribution Law, and we expect that for years to come it will be very difficult to predict the outcome of a New York divorce trial involving a professional license. Some recent New York decisions have held that, where there is a "track record" as to professional earnings, that record should be the basis for valuing a professional practice and that the value of the license merges into the value of the practice.

YOUR STAMP COLLECTION

Specific items of marital property may have great sentimental value to one spouse or the other. The court will attempt to award to each party the items in which he or she has a personal interest, such as sporting goods, tools, and special collections. The court will also try to allocate items that common sense dictates should be awarded to one party: a library used by only one of them, or jewelry worn by the other. In general, the court will take into account the reasonable expressed wishes of each individual.

Some of the questions in the following checklist may be applicable to your own situation. Many of the issues are sophisticated and will, no doubt, require professional assistance to resolve.

CHECKLIST FOR PROPERTY DIVISION

1. If you own a home, who is named on the title? Are there any other parcels of real property or stock ownership in a cooperative corporation? What is the title status? Are there any mortgages, liens, or encumbrances on the title? Who will assume which obligations?

2. Have the taxes been paid? What tax consequences will occur from any transfer of interest in real estate? If property other than real estate is to be sold, what are the tax consequences there? Will an appraiser be required to value the property? Who will pay for the cost of the appraisal?
3. If you are living in a rental apartment, is there a lease? In whose name is it leased? When does the lease expire? Is the building likely to become a cooperative or a condominium? Who is to continue occupying the apartment? Who is to pay the rent? Is the lease assignable? Is it to be assigned? If there is a deposit, who is to receive that?
4. Is it necessary to dispose of a business? If so, should the value of the business be appraised? Is the business a partnership? Is the spouse a partner? If so, is that interest to be purchased by the other spouse? Is the business incorporated? Are both spouses officers or directors? Is one to resign? If both are stockholders, what disposition is to be made of the holdings? If one is a creditor, what disposition is to be made of that claim?
5. Does the business or professional practice have goodwill value? Did either spouse acquire a professional license during the marriage? How should the goodwill or the license be valued?
6. Is one spouse holding in his/her name any separate property belonging to the other spouse? If so, is he/she to retain it?
7. Is there any insurance on personal items: jewelry, furs, cameras, etc.? Are any of the policies to be transferred?
8. Does either of the parties have an interest in any profit sharing plans, pension plans, or other retirement funds? Are they fully or partially vested? Will an actuary be required? What disposition is to be made of these interests? Why?
9. Does either spouse owe the other any money? Is there an outstanding note or other evidence of the debt? How is the indebtedness to be treated?
10. Are you and your spouse jointly liable on any obligation? If so, what happens when the obligation matures? Is one spouse to assume the debt and indemnify the other?
11. Is there any litigation pending between the spouses in addition to the divorce proceeding? Is there any other pending litigation in which one or both of you are involved, either as a plaintiff or as a defendant?

Property Division 99

12. Are there any outstanding bills or obligations that were incurred by one spouse, but for which the other is or may be liable? Who is to discharge that obligation? Is there to be indemnification?
13. When should credit cards and accounts be canceled and surrendered? Can each spouse's credit be preserved by opening new accounts?
14. Are schedules to be prepared, listing exact debts each spouse is to assume and pay?
15. Have the parties filed any joint income tax returns in the past? If there is a refund, who is to get it? If there is a deficiency assessment, who is to pay it? Is one spouse to indemnify the other as to any liability regarding prior income tax returns?
16. Who is responsible for other tax matters, such as estate taxes, corporation returns, and partnership returns?
17. Are authenticated copies of future tax returns to be exchanged?
18. Is each party to waive his or her rights in the estate of the other?
19. Has either party an existing will in which the other is named executor or executrix, devisee, or legatee? Should this be changed?
20. Should either spouse be required to leave the other or the children a specific sum or sums by will or is that spouse's estate to be charged for future support, medical obligations, etc.?
21. Are there revocable "living trusts" that should be changed because of the altered marital relationship?
22. Are the children beneficiaries under any existing testamentary or living trusts? Should they be? Which parent is to receive and control the income on the children's behalf?
23. Is the spouse's maintenance obligation (assuming there are continuing payments) to survive death and be binding upon his/her estate? If so, may the obligation be capitalized so that the estate may be promptly closed?
24. Is a spouse to furnish any security for the performance of his/her obligations under the agreement? If so, what form will the security take?

CHAPTER SEVEN
SPOUSAL MAINTENANCE

UNTIL 1980, New York statutes permitted awards of alimony only to "innocent" wives who had not committed acts that gave their husbands fault grounds for divorce. Husbands could not get alimony regardless of the circumstances. Only in a non-divorce situation in Family Court was it theoretically possible to impose a support obligation on a wife, in order to keep the husband off public assistance.

In addition to the alimony-is-only-for-wives characteristic of New York law before 1980, it was more difficult for husbands than it was for wives, under comparable circumstances, to obtain a divorce on fault grounds such as adultery, abandonment, or cruelty, especially if the marriage had been of long duration (about eighteen or twenty years). New York Courts made fault divorces harder for husbands to get because a fault divorce against the wife meant she couldn't get alimony whatever her need.

The enactment of the Equitable Distribution Law, which became effective July 19, 1980, changed much of that. "Maintenance," the new term for alimony, was formerly awarded primarily on the economic basis of reasonable needs and ability to pay. The 1986 amendment to the 1980 statute, however, shifted some emphasis to the standard of living maintained during the marriage. It may be awarded to a husband, as well as to a wife, and may be permanent or temporary. The marital fault of a wife no longer is an automatic bar to alimony; now only behavior so bad that it shocks the court's conscience is relevant in awarding maintenance (or in the distribution of marital property). The new law requires the divorce court to consider 11 factors (similar to but not the same as the 13 factors used in dividing marital property) in deciding the amount and duration of maintenance. Those factors are listed in Appendix B on page 229, under number 6, "Maintenance." Back to Mary Ellen.

EACH SPOUSE IS FINANCIALLY RESPONSIBLE FOR THE OTHER

"Does alimony still exist?" Mary Ellen wanted to know. We explained that over the years the term alimony developed a negative connotation, and it has been replaced by the less-charged term: maintenance. Whatever it is called, it represents monetary support to the needy spouse. However, the concept of support that will last indefinitely, which was the general rule for wives under the pre-1980 law in New York, has fallen from favor. The 11 factors the court is directed to evaluate in deciding whether to award maintenance, and for how long and how much, emphasize the rehabilitative and temporary aspects, unless there is dependency.

In the past, the norm was for the woman to be the homemaker and the man the breadwinner. Today, when over half of the women between the ages of eighteen and sixty-two are working outside the home, the trend—not only in New York, but throughout the country—is to award lower spousal maintenance over a shorter period of time. And, of course, alimony or maintenance statutes cannot be sexually discriminatory, as they were in New York before the Equitable Distribution Law, and husbands can now sue for maintenance, although they rarely do. Mary Ellen was correct when she assumed she needed to return to the job market, because the purpose of spousal maintenance for younger wives is generally considered to be rehabilitative in nature, not a lifetime annuity. Simply stated, the court may limit support to the period that is necessary for Mary Ellen to become self-supporting at a level the court considers adequate. If Mary Ellen could not become capable of earning enough to meet her own financial needs, then the court might require her husband to pay maintenance permanently.

TEMPORARY SUPPORT AND MAINTENANCE

Mary Ellen was understandably frightened when Jim reluctantly packed his bags and left. They had not yet made provisions for her financial support. She realized this oversight was caused by the unusual circumstances of Jim's departure, but she feared being left without money for the duration of the divorce proceedings. She honestly had no idea how she would maintain the house and feed the two children and herself without Jim's paycheck safely deposited in their checking account.

Fortunately, the courts can intervene if one spouse is left with insufficient funds during the divorce proceedings. Temporary support during the divorce action is designed to maintain the status quo as nearly as possible while the divorce is pending. The court has discretion to consider some or none of the 11 statutory factors in setting temporary maintenance, pending trial. Your lawyer can obtain an Order to Show Cause and a subsequent Temporary Order, which will provide temporary payments until the final decree. The temporary support will rarely be enough to maintain the former standard of living. Mary Ellen did not require an accountant's expertise to realize that Jim's income must now provide for two homes, their respective living expenses, and two lawyers. It was unlikely that she would receive as much for household expenses as she had been receiving prior to the separation. Courts will not impoverish the supporting spouse, or he may just stop working. Rather, judges seek to leave both spouses with a fair share of the available resources to cover necessary living expenses.

FROM EACH ACCORDING TO HIS OR HER ABILITY

The husband's and wife's relative earning capacities and needs, the primary determinants of the term and amount of maintenance, are a function of many factors. Despite many advances in women's access to jobs in the past twenty years, women who work outside the home still tend to be in lower-paying job categories than men. Employed women with college degrees earn, on an average, less than the average for men with no more than an eighth-grade education. Mary Ellen had a college degree, but her work experience was limited, as were job opportunities in her particular field of teaching. Although educational level and work experience contribute to earning capacity, the courts will use discretion before assuming employability. A degree in history or a job as a clerk/typist fourteen years ago does not place one in high demand in today's job market. An award of spousal maintenance may be designed specifically to train the supported spouse for better employment through a return to college or a trade school.

Ability of the husband to pay necessarily limits the amount of support and even the possibility of providing support. To determine Jim's ability to pay, Mary Ellen and I looked at their tax returns for the last two years. Next we studied her accounts of their living expenses prior to separation. This helped establish the dollar needs of both parties. Only after deducting Jim's fixed expenses—rent, food, car, and medical—could we get an idea of what we might ask for support.

If your spouse's income comes from his or her privately owned business, you will probably need an accountant. Perhaps many private expenses are incurred by the business for tax purposes rather than being distributed as personal income. Of course, it is to the owner-spouse's advantage to show a limited income. Obviously, the less income produced, the less money is available for spousal maintenance!

TO EACH ACCORDING TO HIS OR HER NEED

Longer marriages, where the woman was the homemaker, yield her relatively greater possibilities for permanent support. Besides having invested a number of years in her husband, the wife will be older and will likely have less current work experience. These last two factors limit her capacity to be self-supporting. A woman under forty is much more likely to find employment than a woman over fifty. Whereas the younger woman may be awarded support and maintenance on a declining scale for a fixed period of time until she is employed and self-supporting, the older woman has a higher likelihood of being granted support until she remarries or receives social security.

The courts often consider the number and ages of the children involved. Perhaps it will be decided that it serves the best interests of the children for the mother to remain home rather than find outside work. This often occurs when the wife has custody of children of preschool age. Nonetheless, over half of the mothers of preschoolers are in the job market.

If health is a primary issue in seeking spousal maintenance, be prepared to substantiate the claim. It may be necessary to support the spouse's claim of health problems with expert medical testimony. This, of course, would apply to either spouse: a wife who seeks support, or a husband who claims that his ill health will reduce his future earning capacity.

Maintenance awards in New York divorce decrees are made in conjunction with property divisions. The courts consider the obligations and assets of both parties, including their separate property and the extent of marital property awarded to each spouse, when deciding about maintenance. The court, as well as the parties, is concerned about the total financial package.

With the court in each case applying the often conflicting statutory factors, there are no simple formulas adequate for predicting spousal maintenance. Our files contain many types of maintenance awards. The bottom line, of course, is individual circumstances. Wealthier clients may obtain $5,000 a month or more; other clients accept awards of $500 or less. Often maintenance payments decline in specified annual amounts on the theory that the dependent spouse should start becoming financially independent, but note that federal tax laws penalize maintenance reductions of more than $15,000 from one year to another during the first three years after maintenance begins.

AVOIDING SPOUSAL MAINTENANCE

It follows that the spouse wishing to avoid paying spousal maintenance will employ all the factors that apply to need, but to his or her own advantage. For example, a husband may try to disprove need, by establishing that his spouse has sufficient funds available to support herself. Perhaps he will attempt to prove she is presently employable or will argue that she could liquidate the marital property she will receive and live off interest and dividend payments. If immediate quality employment is not possible, he may maintain that suitable training can be obtained in less time and for less expense than she claims is required. In this case, he may need to employ experts in employment counseling to corroborate his claim.

If the financially stronger spouse cannot establish that the other can and should take care of herself financially, he may attempt to prove that he cannot pay what she does need. He may assert living expenses of his own, which deny or sharply limit the funds available for support. He may point to factors that reduce or limit his future earning ability. Obviously, the respective financial needs and abilities to pay of the spouses require careful investigation and balancing.

ATTORNEY FEES

There may be a question of responsibility for attorney fees. The law does not entitle either spouse to free litigation. A genuine need must exist before the law will require one spouse to pay the other's attorney fees. A disparity in income is not reason enough for the wealthier spouse to accept the responsibility. The award of attorney fees must be based on the honest financial need of one party and the ability of the other party to pay.

MAINTENANCE IN THE SETTLEMENT AGREEMENT

A well-drafted separation or settlement agreement guards against future problems and should help to eliminate the need for later modification. Therefore, your attorney needs answers for the following questions before drafting your settlement agreement:

SPOUSAL MAINTENANCE CHECKLIST

1. If there are to be maintenance payments, are they fixed in amount or subject to fluctuation? How much do they decline in value? What factors cause fluctuation?
2. When are the support payments to be made? On what dates?
3. To whom are the support payments to be made? What are the penalties if they are late?
4. Can the spouse obtain income from employment or some other source, without affecting the amount of the support allowance? If so, is there to be any limitation on the amount that can be earned?
5. When does the allowance to the spouse end?
6. How are the spouse's social security rights to be handled? What benefits?
7. What are the tax consequences of the payments? If maintenance payments total more than $15,000 per year, there are rules under the Tax Reform Act of 1986 that must be carefully observed. If those rules are not followed, what are intended to be maintenance payments may become nondeductible to the paying spouse and nontaxable to the receiving spouse.
8. Are there to be security provisions, such as a bond, to guarantee the payments?
9. Who is to pay the parties' respective attorney's fees and costs of suit? How much? When?
10. Can the tax laws be properly applied to make attorney's fees legally deductible? Can the form of billing assist in a tax savings?
11. Who pays for audits, costs of transferring real estate, and other expenses incident to the dissolution of the marriage?

Spousal Maintenance

12. Is one party to pay the other party's attorney's fees and costs arising out of any post-judgment litigation? Under what terms and conditions is the party responsible?
13. Is cohabitation a reason for termination of support?
14. Is remarriage a reason for termination of support?

CHAPTER EIGHT
CHILD SUPPORT

Parents have a legal obligation to furnish financial support to their children in accordance with their abilities and the circumstances. A court in setting child support is required by New York law in effect at this writing to consider:

1. the financial resources of the custodial and noncustodial parent, and those of the child
2. the physical and emotional health of the child, and his or her educational or vocational needs and aptitudes
3. where practical and relevant, the standard of living the child would have enjoyed had the marriage not been dissolved
4. where practical and relevant, the tax consequences to the parties; and
5. the nonmonetary contributions that the parents will make toward the care and well-being of the child

New York, as well as all other states, is required under a 1984 federal statute to create and have in its law by October 1, 1987 quantifiable guidelines for setting child support amounts. In accordance with the federal mandate, Governor Cuomo has proposed legislation that, if it became law, would replace the five general factors listed above with a "child support formula" in

Child Support

determining support. The formula is complex, in keeping with New York's legislative traditions. The above five factors would be used only if the judge determined that variance from the amount given under the "child support formula" was appropriate in the specific case.

Appendix D is exerpts from the Governor's bill as presented in 1986, including two tables which define parents' combined contributions for child support where they have two children. The tables correlate the parents' "combined marginal income" and the parents' combined "support obligation", and distinguish between the needs of children aged 0-11 and children aged 12-21.

The child support guidelines which become law may be different from those given in the proposal excerpted in Appendix D, but it is certain that some guidelines will become effective in New York during 1987. Accordingly, our discussion of the existing child support law below is brief and general.

BOTH PARENTS ARE RESPONSIBLE

Today New York courts recognize the obligation of both parents to provide for the support of their children until the age of twenty-one. Each parent will be required to discharge the obligation in accordance with his/her capacity and ability. Thus, when the support order is considered, the court will determine what, if any, contribution each spouse should provide. This principle will probably not change under any child support guidelines legislation. It should be remembered that the children are not parties to a parental agreement regarding their support. Courts are free to disregard agreements that are detrimental to the children and to increase or decrease the level for their support. The chief legal effect of such agreements, if any, is in the allocation of the support duty as between parents, but the welfare of the children may require a court to override such allocations.

COST OF LIVING INCREASES

Support awards become outdated. As children grow, so do their needs. In addition, inflation can be expected to eat away the value of the support award. Many of the separation agreements we prepare contain cost of living provisions, which are based upon the Consumer Price Index. The idea of CPI "escalators" is to maintain the real value of the child support at its intended level as inflation erodes the buying power of the original dollar amount. Often the parent paying child support will insist on a "de-escalator" so that dollar payments will be permitted to decline if deflation should increase the buying power of the original support amount. The bottom line is that the parents are required to provide "adequate" child support, and the amount, therefore, is subject to modification due to changed circumstances.

DURATION OF SUPPORT

Beyond the dollar amount of child support and the inclusion of escalation clauses, consideration must be given to the duration of support in a separation agreement between the parents. Mary Ellen and Jim both agreed that the children should attend college and were prepared to provide for graduate school if it was warranted. Jim had always hoped that Justin would become a doctor, and that he might need help with educational expenses well after he was twenty-one. Jim assured both us and his own attorney that he had every intention of providing college and graduate school education for his children at least until the age of twenty-three, and that promise was included in the separation agreement. Some parents share the costs of college equally; others share ratably in accordance with their respective ability to contribute. Perhaps the children may be expected to contribute as well.

ENFORCEMENT

Recent legislation, both federal and New York State, has greatly increased the ability of the parent due child support, usually the mother, to collect. In particular, the New York State Enforcement Act of 1986 has both streamlined and strengthened the systems available to custodial parents.

A parent can now make effective use, with or without an attorney, of family court and its hearing examiners to get a court order defining the child support due from the other parent. If the court order is not obeyed, it is easier for the custodial parent to garnish the wages of the non-custodial parent, to obtain a money judgment for child support arrears and to use other enforcement mechanisms that it was a few years ago. Nonetheless, failure to pay child support when due and in the amount required by the court is still a very serious problem.

SUPPORT IN THE SEPARATION AGREEMENT

The following questions may help when considering support provisions. A separation agreement need not necessarily be comprehensive and detailed enough to answer all these questions; hopefully the parents will retain an ability to communicate and agree on reasonable solutions as they are needed.

Support Checklist

1. How often and on what dates are the support payments to be made?
2. Are support payments reduced or waived in part during periods when the children are visiting with the noncustodial parent, when living away at school or at summer camp, or when the noncustodial parent contributes to daycare expenses? If so, by how much?
3. Are child support provisions to be designated as such in the separation agreement, or are they to be lumped together with the maintenance allowance for the spouse? (Tax consequences of this could be severe and should be discussed with the lawyer.)
4. Is there a specific amount allocated to each child?
5. Who claims which child as a dependent for income tax purposes? Under what terms and conditions will the parent claim the children? What is the value of this exemption to each parent in after-tax dollars?
6. Are the payments to continue in whole or in part when the children become emancipated? Under what terms and conditions and how?
7. Will support continue through college? Will it include college expenses?
8. Can the parent in charge of custody obtain income from employment or some other source without affecting the amount of child support he receives? If so, is there to be any limitation?
9. Is the custodial parent to receive any supplemental support for such expenses as summer camp, religious training, music lessons, or other special expenses?
10. Who pays for the *ordinary* medical, dental, and optical expenses for the children?
11. Who pays for the *extraordinary* medical, dental, optical, and related expenses of the children? Which hospital, optical, orthodontia, dental, medical, surgical, counseling, or psychiatric expenses should be classified as extraordinary? Will this include family counseling expenses?
12. Is there any notice to be given to the noncustodial parent before extraordinary medical, dental, orthodontia, or optical expenses are incurred? If so, how much notice?

13. Who chooses the doctor, dentist, or other specialist?
14. Is medical insurance to be maintained? Who will pay for the insurance? What is the minimum extent of coverage to be provided? What evidence of coverage is to be given?
15. Are any medical, dental, optical, or related payments to be continued beyond the time a child reaches majority? Will it continue during the time a child attends trade school, college, or professional school?
16. Who pays the trade school or college tuition fees of the children? Who pays for graduate school, professional school, other special school?
17. Who decides what school the children will attend, the location of the school, checks the accreditation of the school?
18. What scholastic performance level must the children maintain?
19. Is there a time limit by which the trade school or college education, graduate school, professional school must be completed?
20. Who pays for room, board, fraternity or sorority, money allowance, and other expenses incidental to the children's education?
21. Who pays for travel expenses to and from school? Is there any limit to the number of trips per school year?
22. Must children apply for loans, scholarships, or school employment?
23. Must children carry a full academic program? Are grade records to be made available to the noncustodial parent?
24. Is there an effect on support if children have income from employment?
25. May college expenses be paid directly to the children?
26. What is the effect of the child's dropping out of school (leave of absence) and later returning? What about the child's marriage before finishing school?

CHAPTER NINE

CHILD CUSTODY

NEW YORK law provides that neither the mother nor the father has a *prima facie* right to custody of the children. Both parents theoretically start as equals when they each ask a court for sole custody of their child. The court is to consider the best interests of the child and to award custody as "justice requires." The parent who is not awarded custody ordinarily will be given reasonable visitation rights.

Under present New York law, the court seldom awards joint legal custody to parents who do not both agree that there should be joint custody. The theory is that if they can't agree that they want joint custody, they will not agree on the many decisions necessary for actually raising the child.

THE CHILDREN SHOULD NOT BE USED AS WEAPONS

Even though the children are not a proper subject for barter, they are sometimes used by either or both parents to obtain bargaining leverage. Each parent has a legally equal chance to win custody, though mothers usually get custody, particularly of younger children. Even so, a threat to fight in court for sole custody may be used to obtain better financial terms for a husband who in actuality is ambivalent about wanting sole legal and physical responsibility for his children. He has something of value to give his wife, his legal right to seek custody, in exchange for something of perhaps great economic value to him. Conversely, if the wife has much the better chance of winning sole custody, should the court be forced to choose between the parties, the husband, who really wants agreed joint custody, may give up a lot financially to win his wife's agreement, rather than risk losing a custody fight?

It is always a relief if and when a client says positively that there will be no custody battle. A fight between parents, which allows the children to become the spoils of war, takes a tragic emotional toll on all the parties, particularly the children. With the diminished importance of marital fault in the divorce process, the litigation opportunities for spouses to express their negative feelings for each other have been narrowed. Where divorce litigation in New York once focused on what miserable and inhumane conduct by the other spouse justified granting a divorce, the focus today is on substantive issues: Who gets the house? What will the support payments be? Who gets the children? Thus conflict over custody of the children can become a primary battleground between spouses who have not completed their psychological divorce.

MAKING THE CUSTODY DECISION

Before parents become embroiled in the custody issue, some serious questions must be answered. Do you *really* want sole custody? Will it serve your children's needs? Too often parents have a knee-jerk reaction about custody. Each seeks custody and endures a legal fight because it is socially expected, and they want to prove to the world how much they care about their children. Or, perhaps, a father lacking in parenting interests seeks custody out of spite, or because his ego has been bruised. Before plunging into a potentially destructive custody battle, consider your motives. Are you battling to protect your interest or those of your children?

The parents' decision should be prompted by the best interests of the children. Consider what you will have to offer your children, both emotionally and financially. What can your spouse offer? Can you cope with the demands of single parenting? How solid is your relationship with your children? What do your children want?

If the custody issue is left to the discretion of the court, the judge will assume the responsibility with great solemnity. The decision will be made according to his or her value system, not yours.

THE NEW YORK STANDARD

New York judges decide custody disputes based upon the best interest of the child, and in doing so consider such factors as:

- the age and sex of the child
- the child's needs and the parent's situation and qualifications
- the number of children and their interrelationship (courts are generally reluctant to split up siblings without good reason, especially if they are young)
- the child's present adjustment to his or her home, school, and community
- the mental and physical health of all individuals involved
- the child's own preference, if the court finds that the child is of sufficient age and discretion

New York State's highest court summarized our custody law in 1984 as follows:

"The only absolute in the law governing custody of children is that there are no absolutes. The Legislature has so declared in directing that custody be determined by the circumstances of the case and of the parties and the best interests of the child, but then adding 'In all cases there shall be no *prima facie* right to the custody of the child in either parent.'"

Inform your lawyer of everything that you believe has a bearing on the custody choice. Tell your lawyer of any appointments your family has had with a social worker, psychiatrist, psychologist, or counselor. Also alert your lawyer if either you or your spouse has ever lost custody of a child before and under what circumstances this occurred.

THE CHILD'S PREFERENCE

It may be difficult to answer the question of whether the child truly prefers to live with you or with the other parent. In New York the preference of older children (at least eleven or twelve years of age) may be considered by the judge if custody is contested. Although judges are reluctant to permit children to testify, many will interview the child in private and may also require expert testimony from psychologists or psychiatrists skilled in interviewing children. Judges realize that children often hesitate to make any comments for fear of alienating either parent.

The court, upon consent of the parties, will refer custody disputes to family counseling units maintained by the court to investigate custodial arrangements and to make recommendations. The social worker will interview the parties directly involved, as well as any physicians, psychologists, or other professionals whom these parties may have seen. The social worker may also choose to refer the child and the parents to professional personnel for diagnosis. The process may become a form of mediation for the parents, in which they have meetings with the social worker and try to reach agreement on a custody and visitation scheme that works for them and their child. As mentioned in the Divorce Mediation chapter, California has had compulsory mediation for child custody disputes since 1981, and there are proposals for similar legislation in New York. If the parents do not agree on custody during the counseling process, the social worker prepares a report with recommendations and sends it to the court.

WHICH PARENT IS MORE FIT?

After examining all the reports, the judge will make a decision concerning the fitness of the parents. The judge's guidelines include both emotional and physical health, as well as the traditional moral fitness. Generally, the court labels both parents as fit even though only one of the parents will be awarded custody. In theory, the court should concern itself only with morality, including sexual morality, that truly affects a parent's relationship with the children.

Fathers' bids for sole custody of their children are no longer uncommon. A 1981 study found that 1.5 million single fathers were raising 3.5 million children. A landmark case involving Dr. Lee Salk, brother of Dr. Jonas Salk of polio vaccine fame, was tried in New York in 1975 and changed the nature of paternal custody challenges nationally. Prior to that decision, a father was encouraged to fight for his children only if he could prove the mother *unfit*. Traditionally, the father's lawyer would pursue a line of questioning to establish extreme misconduct on the part of the mother: child abuse, alcoholism, prostitution. If negative behavior could not be attributed to the mother, the father was advised to forget about custody.

The Salk case took two years to resolve, but ultimately the father won custody of his children, aged two, six, and twelve, even though the court found that both parties loved the children and that both were fit parents. This case encouraged Jim in his custody effort. He was confident that any court would affirm both Mary Ellen and himself as fit parents but, like Dr. Salk, he hoped to prove himself to be the *more* fit parent.

Whether the court decides custody or the parents mediate and draft their own contract, the custody agreement is a matter of great importance. Generally, the parent with legal custody has the right to determine the children's upbringing. This includes education, health care, and religious training as well as such day-to-day decisions as bedtime, enrichment programs, and visits to the doctor. In effect, the custodial parent is given control of the children's lives, while the noncustodial parent's rights and responsibilities are limited to those listed in the decree. However, parents who are able to communicate with one another about the children may find it advantageous to agree to joint responsibilities for their upbringing. Joint custody agreements commonly name both parents responsible for education, summer plans, health care, and general welfare.

CUSTODY MODIFICATION

Custody decrees always remain subject to modification if the court finds that circumstances warrant this, though a court is naturally reluctant to disturb settled custody arrangements, particularly where the prior custody determination was made recently or after a full trial. Just what circumstances will justify a change in custody may vary from judge to judge. New York's highest court in 1984 stated that extraordinary circumstances are not necessary for a change in parental custody, and that the best interests of the child should determine custody modification, just as they have governed a court's initial custody determination. Custody modification will reflect the values and biases of the judge and the community just as the original award did. The child's welfare depends in part on the continuity and stability of his home life, and the court will not change custody unless it finds that a change will truly benefit the child.

Some fact patterns encourage custody modification. One such situation is deliberate frustration or interference with the noncustodial parent's visitation rights. New York courts in several cases have refused to permit a custodial mother to move away from New York with her children, when her reason to move was not strong enough and when the children's being far away from New York would frustrate the father's visitation rights.

Another situation that calls for custody modification is child abuse or neglect. Any situation that threatens the child's physical or mental health will be viewed with concern by the court. This includes overt physical abuse and more subtle cases in which the parent consistently places his or her own interests well above those of the child—for example, cases where the custodial parent's lifestyle is inconsistent with important needs of the child.

Remarriage cannot, in itself, result in modification of the custody award. Most divorced parents do, in fact, remarry, and in many cases the child benefits from the new relationship with the stepparent. If, however, there arise within the new family difficulties that threaten the child's welfare, the court may modify the custody. For example, if the child and the stepparent are very hostile to one another, with little hope of improvement, or if the child's relationship with stepsiblings is so poor that it affects his or her emotional well-being, the court may change custody to the other parent. Modification should occur only if there is a change in the circumstances of the child or the custodial parent. A change in the circumstances of the noncustodial parent is rarely sufficient reason for modification.

Common sense tells us that sometimes the parents themselves find it necessary to modify custody. The courts recognize this need. If parents can reach agreement with one another in good faith, then, of course, they are the best judges of what is right for the children, and the courts will not interfere. However, a parent should never agree to a change of custody under coercion or threat from the other parent.

THE COLD WAR: VIOLATING THE DECREE

Even after the ordeal of hammering out an agreement and fighting for custody, there are parents who will continue the fight by violating the provisions of the decree. Violations range in severity. It may be only the custodial parent's failure, whether unconscious and innocent or deliberate, to have the children ready at the agreed time for the other's visit. Although that is aggravating, there are far more flagrant violations. Deliberate violations of the custody provision can make life miserable for both the children and the parents. Serious, ongoing violations may merit such disapproval that the court will change the custody arrangement entirely.

Too often, parents use custody provisions to continue their war with each other. The visiting parent will repeatedly keep the children out late on the days spent together. The custodial parent will refuse visitation privileges because the monthly support check has not arrived. Besides being in violation of the decree, these tactics are clearly not in the children's best interests. Do not threaten your spouse with denial of rights given him or her in the custody decree. Besides being illegal, such threats may backfire and jeopardize your legal status with regard to your children.

What causes these infuriating violations? Perhaps the first action you should take is to examine your particular problem. You may be able to stop the violations if you determine that your own conduct is part of the problem. What is your reaction when the other parent consistently returns the children two hours late on visiting days? Do you rant and rave? It is entirely possible that your ex-spouse is playing a power game with you by deliberately flouting the visitation schedule in order to manipulate you and provoke conflict. If you respond in a low-key, emotionally relaxed manner, instead of over-reacting, he/she may realize the manipulative tactic is not working and give it up.

If you cannot obtain the cooperation of the other parent in stopping violations, you should consult your attorney. The lawyers of both parties can then confer and perhaps reach a resolution of the situation. It is possible that your spouse's lawyer will be able to persuade him or her to cease the aggravating conduct. If not, you have the option of returning to court. Court-imposed remedies for custody violations will include an injunction ordering the offending parent to refrain from particular, specified conduct. Violations of the order can result in a finding of contempt, and, in extreme cases, jail time can be imposed. Naturally, it may be difficult to tailor a list of infringements precisely enough to completely cure the situation, and enforcement then becomes an additional problem.

CHILD-SNATCHING

In the past, cases of parents "snatching" or kidnapping their own children and taking them out of the state have been a grave concern to families and courts. At the root of the problem was the willingness of different jurisdictions to reopen custody matters that were originally determined in other states. All fifty states have now adopted the Uniform Child Custody Jurisdiction Act, which was designed to discourage both child-snatching and conflicts between states, by giving deference to the first state's custody determination. The federal Parental Kidnapping Prevention Act of 1980 mandates that state courts honor (give "full faith and credit") to existing custody decrees previously made by another state. That act also makes a federal criminal offense of parental kidnapping and also of interstate or international flight to avoid prosecution under child-snatching felony statutes.

One federal court's civil punishment of a father for child abduction produced a large monetary award to the custodial mother. After a scheduled summer visit with his two children, the father fled with them to Canada. When he was found, the mother sued for damages, and the United States Court of Appeals affirmed the jury's decision to award the mother $130,000. The father and his relatives were found liable for that amount in compensatory and punitive damages for their abduction of the children.

In order to benefit from changes in the law, a parent must first know where the other parent has taken the children. The saddest of such cases involves the parent who has carried out his or her abduction plan in such secrecy that the other parent has no clue to their whereabouts. Unless information can be obtained from friends or relatives, the custodial parent may be helpless. Police and other law enforcement officials usually will not help beyond the borders of their own jurisdiction and, in any case, are often reluctant to be drawn into domestic matters. Thus, unless the parent can afford to hire the services of a private detective, he or she faces a desperate situation without much hope, because the search can become a prohibitively expensive endeavor. However, in the fall of 1982, the FBI computers were opened up to the search for missing children nationwide. This could be a boon to parents of abducted children.

Once again, if you are facing this type of problem, a lawyer's advice is essential to determine your legal recourse. It is also urgent to act immediately. The longer your ex-spouse is gone with the children, the more difficult it will be to trace them.

Answering the following list of questions before the final decree will reduce the potential for future conflicts on custodial issues. Combine these questions with those following the "Visitation" and "Joint Custody" chapters to guide you in developing a specific list for your own situation.

CUSTODY CHECKLIST

1. Which parent will make decisions governing the choice of schools, doctors, dentists, surgeons? Is the other parent to be consulted?
2. Which parent is to make decisions concerning summer plans: camps, trips, etc.? Is the other parent to be consulted?
3. Which parent is to make decisions in regard to religious training?
4. In the event of a dispute, is there to be arbitration, or will you need to resort to a court for a decision?
5. May the children be permanently moved to another jurisdiction? Must the custodial parent first obtain permission from a court? Is there to be any notice to the noncustodial parent? How much notice should the noncustodial parent be given?
6. If the child is moved to another jurisdiction, how will the visitation provisions be adjusted?
7. Who will pay the transportation expenses for long-distance visitation?
8. What will be the frequency of telephone contact with the children? If telephone contact involves a long-distance fee, who will be responsible for the bill?
9. Is there to be any notice to the noncustodial parent, in the event a child becomes seriously ill or injured? Will the doctor be directed to make all information available to the other parent?
10. If the mother remarries, can the children's surname be changed to that of the stepfather? What are the remedies open to the father?
11. Are the children to have any voice in any decision pertaining to their custody? At what age?

CHAPTER TEN

JOINT CUSTODY

MANY DIVORCING parents are questioning the traditional sole custody system, where one parent has sole legal responsibility for the child while, the other parent has visitation rights and obligations to pay support. Those parents want to *share,* after divorce, the problems, costs, privileges, and responsibilities of raising their children, more equally than is possible in the rigid "weekend Daddy" formulas often set by courts. Such parents may opt for joint custody, also commonly described as shared custody or co-parenting. Their exact numbers are unknown, but we believe that about 15 percent of the divorced parents of the United States currently have a shared custody arrangement.

Shared custody often includes arrangements for the child to reside with each parent for alternating periods so that the child in effect has two homes. Shared *physical* custody is not essential, however, to the concept of shared *legal* custody. Critics of shared custody often focus on the logistics problems. It may, therefore, be advisable to separate the legal concept from its day-to-day reality in order to evaluate its merit.

THE LEGAL CONCEPT

At a minimum, shared custody means that both parents have a legal responsibility for raising the child and making decisions about his or her education, health care, and general welfare. It is a type of custody in which the parents need to maintain good contact with each other after divorce; they must cooperate to make joint decisions about the child's life. Clearly, this will only be effective if the parents can, at least sometimes, calmly and reasonably communicate with one another. If it was not possible in the marriage, it may be unreasonable to assume it will happen after divorce. Symbolically and legally, under joint legal custody both parents have equal rights to raise the child. Neither is granted exclusive power to rear the child, and neither is relegated to the position of visitor.

Joint physical custody includes joint legal custody and also means that the child lives alternatively at each parent's home on a regular basis; for instance, one week at the father's house and the next week at the mother's house. The variations are endless, but the concept is that the child's time is split approximately equally between the parents and applies whether the child's moving cycle is twice a week or once a year.

Joint custody is gaining more acceptance for several reasons, but it seems to be a natural outgrowth of the broadening roles of men and women in our society. Married women no longer automatically stay at home to keep house and take primary responsibility for child-rearing, as was the norm in the 1950s. At the same time, many men are assuming more responsibility at home. They actively seek to share in their children's lives, including the physical caretaking once considered "woman's work." Thus, the traditional sex-role stereotypes of housewife-mother and breadwinner-father are to some extent breaking down.

When such marriages head for divorce, parents naturally seek a custody arrangement reflecting these changing-role developments. The father will not be satisfied with demotion to second-class status with his children, and the mother, with her outside job responsibilities, may not feel able to cope with the burden of single parenting. Shared custody can be a solution.

JOINT CUSTODY: IS IT FOR YOU?

Joint custody is not feasible in all cases. Here are some family characteristics that can contribute to the success of shared custody.

- Each parent should be capable of rearing the child.
- Both parents should accept frequent contact with one another. Especially in the early stages, shared custody involves communication. It requires real effort, cooperation, and frequent readjustment, while working out unforeseen problems.
- Shared custody assumes that the parents have resolved the conflicts between themselves or at least have been able to subordinate them to a common concern for the child.
- Each parent sincerely wants active involvement in the child's life.
- The parents should live in reasonable proximity to each other if they are to share physical custody of the children with approximate equality. They need to live near enough to one another to make the residence changes practicable. Nearness extends to other considerations:
    - *The age of the child:* The younger the child, the less desirable it may be for him or her to move back and forth.
    - *School arrangements:* Both parents should live close to the schools.
    - *Friendships:* Do other family members and close friends live nearby?
    - *Financial resources:* Shifting between residences that are geographically far apart will be difficult if family finances are insufficient.
- Older children should favor a joint custody arrangement or at least not be opposed to it.
- Flexibility in the parents' jobs reduces conflicts. They need time off for the children's medical appointments and parent-teacher conferences. Parents without this flexibility can still make a joint physical custody arrangement work, but it will be difficult. Parents who have committed themselves to share physical custody rather than be content with weekend visitation often find that they must make sacrifices in their careers.
- Were the parents both actively involved in caring for the child

during marriage? This is not an absolute prerequisite, but it clearly makes the transition easier for all concerned.
- Common goals for the children and similar attitudes toward child rearing are crucial. This is really a matter of shared *values*.
- Finally, do you have adequate financial resources? It is a mistake to assume that money alone is enough to make joint custody work, but it helps. Children need love and warmth, which money can't buy; they also need extra clothes if they shuttle frequently between Mom's house and Dad's house. A child may not have to have a separate room in each home to feel he belongs, but having his own adequate space in both homes will help.

JOINT CUSTODY: THE PROS, THE CONS, THE UNKNOWN

Since it is a new phenomenon, joint cutody is still surrounded by controversy. Parents tend to be more receptive to the idea than are lawyers and judges. Indeed, many lawyers try to discourage their clients from seeking joint custody. They warn them that while it sounds nice in theory, it may be impractical in reality for two people split by divorce to agree upon decisions concerning their children's welfare. Therefore, in the name of efficiency, many lawyers recommend the traditional sole custody award. To make an informed decision, you should consider the advantages and disadvantages that are often discussed by experts in the custody area.

THE ADVANTAGES

Besides serving the goal of preserving the parent-child relationship, joint custody offers the following advantages:

1. The most important reason for joint custody is the minimization of psychological harm to the child. The mere fact of divorce probably will harm the child. But when one parent, in effect, divorces his children by giving up meaningful contact with them, the emotional damage is compounded. Most psy-

chologists agree that the gravest harm to children of divorce is the loss of the relationship with one parent. If, as often happens, the noncustodial parent gradually fades from the child's life, the child usually perceives the absence as rejection by that parent. Consequently, the child grows up with low self-esteem, the impression that he or she caused the problem and so is in some way unlovable. Of course, a particularly resilient child, or one with other strong familial support, can overcome the loss, but many, not so fortunate, do not. In cases where both parents are willing to make it work, joint custody may guarantee the ongoing role of each parent in the child's life, thus reducing the child's fears of losing either parent.

2. By dividing physical custody, the parent who would otherwise have sole custody has more time for his or her career and a personal life apart from the children.

3. The child will have fewer problems of divided loyalty in relation to the parents. Neither parent has been dubbed superior, and both have equal authority. Therefore, the child is relieved of the considerable guilt often experienced by him/her in the traditional custody situation. When sole custody is awarded, the child may feel resentment toward the custodial parent for having deprived him or her of the other parent. In addition, the child may accuse the absent parent of desertion, or may fantasize about the absent parent and yearn to live with him or her, thus engendering further guilt about the custodial parent.

4. Joint custody is inherently more flexible than sole custody awards. Because the parents have equal authority before the law, they can readjust custody arrangements as necessary when the family situation changes, without petitioning the court for modification.

5. Joint custody keeps the decision making power with those who best know the needs of the children. It provides decision making without interference by a court.

6. The effort required to make joint custody work provides excellent parental role-models for the children. The child learns that love requires compromise and dedication to the interests of others.

7. Child support money may become less of a problem when both parents are participating actively in the care of the children. The need to transfer funds by monthly check may disap-

pear, as each parent assumes different support costs. At least the parents are likely to be more understanding of each other's needs when they share everyday concerns.

The Disadvantages

Joint custody has some inherent disadvantages. For example:

1. The joint custody arrangement may become an extension of the power struggle between parents who are unable to resolve their conflict.
2. Some children may find it stressful to be shuttled back and forth between two households under joint physical custody. This argument is particularly valid for children under the age of seven or eight.
3. Joint physical custody restricts the mobility of parents because of the need for geographic proximity.
4. It may perpetuate the child's secret hopes for reconciliation of the parents.
5. Joint custody chosen for the wrong reasons may keep the parents from facing up to the reality of divorce.
6. Joint physical custody can be much more expensive because of the need to maintain two homes for the child.

Living Arrangements: Potentially a Major Hurdle

Working out residential arrangements can be a major problem. If the primary goal of shared custody is to preserve and strengthen both parent-child relationships, sharing physical care must be an integral part of the plan. Of course, the age of the child or the distance between residences must be considered. In most cases, some sharing of physical custody is planned for. The big consideration lies in working out living arrangements that are not too burdensome or disruptive to the child's life.

In joint custody there can be a wide variety of residential patterns. In some families the child stays half the week with one parent, then goes to the other parent for the rest of the week. In other cases the child alternates residences weekly, or perhaps monthly. There have even been cases in which the child lives for an entire year with one parent, then goes to the other parent for a year. Depending on the circumstances of those involved, each of these arrangements could be acceptable or otherwise, but they indicate the range of possibilities.

In a few families the children do not switch residences, the parents do. Thus, after each interval designated in the agreement, one parent leaves the central residence and the other parent comes in. Maintaining three households can be quite expensive. One suburban family manages a variation of this theme. The children reside in the "family" home. The parents share, on a rotating basis, an apartment in the city. Each parent spends two weeks with the children in the suburbs while the other parent lives in the city.

Clearly these arrangements would not appeal to all adults, but they may provide stability in the children's lives. They do show that great flexibility and imagination can be used in working out a satisfactory joint custody arrangement.

As mentioned previously, when children have two residences it is important that there be a sense of belonging at each place. The child should at least have his own corner, a place for toys and a few clothes, if not a separate bedroom. Most of all, the children need to know that both parents want them and look forward to being with and caring for them, for that is the heart of joint custody or shared parenting after divorce.

It cannot be too much emphasized that a constant and sensitive awareness of the children's situation is a major responsibility for everyone—parents, lawyers, mediators, the courts—involved in a divorce action. Please read carefully the following Bill of Rights for Children, prepared by the staff of the Family Court Counseling Service of Dane County, Wisconsin.

BILL OF RIGHTS FOR CHILDREN OF DIVORCE

1. The right to be treated as important human beings, with unique feelings, ideas, and desires, and not as a source of argument between parents.
2. The right to a continuing relationship with both parents and the freedom to receive love from and express love for both.
3. The right to express love and affection for each parent without having to stifle that love because of fear of disapproval by the other parent.
4. The right to know that their parents' decision to divorce is not their responsibility and that they will live with one parent and will visit the other parent.
5. The right to continuing care and guidance from both parents.
6. The right to honest answers to questions about the changing family relationships.
7. The right to know and appreciate what is good in each parent without one parent degrading the other.
8. The right to have a relaxed, secure relationship with both parents without being placed in a position to manipulate one parent against the other.
9. The right to have the custodial parent not undermine visitation by suggesting tempting alternatives or by threatening to withhold visitation as a punishment for the children's wrongdoing.
10. The right to be able to experience regular and consistent visitation, and the right to know the reason for a canceled visit.

CHAPTER ELEVEN

VISITATION

DESPITE THE option of joint physical custody most divorces leave one parent, usually the mother, with primary physical custody of the children. Visitation by the other parent, usually the father, is probably one of the least carefully considered provisions of most divorce agreements and decrees. This is unfortunate because visitation can be one of the most frequent areas of post-divorce conflict. Visitation plans should be created to maintain the bonding between each parent and child. It can make the difference between a child who feels loved and secure and a child who feels the loss of one parent and lives in fear of losing the other.

Too often parents and their lawyers inappropriately fall back on the broad standard set by statute, which simply provides that the parent who does not have legal custody shall have "reasonable visitation." The divorcing parents are often so relieved to reach agreement in other areas that they are unwilling to delay the proceedings over visitation and assume that visitation will work out after the emotional friction has dissipated. Lawyers know that this friction sometimes does not dissipate and that visitation, as a remaining tie between parents after divorce, can become a new battlefield.

WORK OUT THE SPECIFICS OF VISITATION

In this working chapter, which has been designed to help you with the actual structuring of visitation, there are sample visitation provisions for your consideration. Of course you must use your own judgment in determining the visitation provisions you would like to have in your decree. In some cases, conflict between the parents creates a need to account for every contingency. Other parents do not require much detail at all. But common sense tells us that a detailed agreement will help create a smooth transition in the initial stages of visitation. A provision merely for "reasonable visitation" invites disagreement as to interpretation.

Consider, for example, the case of Janet and Bruce, whose children were preschoolers when they divorced. The divorce left both parents with pain and bitterness. Janet got sole custody of the children by agreement. Then, with no real guidance, they simply agreed to reasonable visitation, with no further description.

As things worked out, Janet thwarted almost all of Bruce's attempts to see the children. She relied upon the common excuse that the kids were sick or that seeing Bruce just did not fit into their schedule. She was still feeling hurt, and this was the only way she knew to inflict pain on Bruce. Consequently, he did not see the children on a regular basis. After all, what is the definition of reasonable visitation? Bruce knew that any interaction with Janet created friction and further harm to the children, so he did not press his visitation rights. Instead, he concentrated on establishing a new single life for himself.

Time passed and the wounds of divorce began to heal. The children were enrolled in school and Janet found herself working. Coping with single parenthood and work was often a burden. Janet now felt the need to share some of the responsibilities or, at least, to have an occasional weekend to herself. Bruce, however, was by now uncomfortable in the role of a parent. He had learned early in the divorce that his presence was not particularly welcome, so the new life he built for himself did not include parenting. The children really didn't know how to relate to him, although the son in particular wanted a close relationship with his father. Janet hoped Bruce would eventually take the children on a regular basis, but so far this has not happened.

Recently, their son, John, talked about his feelings. He said, "When they got divorced I was only five and I really didn't know what was going on. But now I'm 12 and Mom treats me like the man of the house or something. It's a lot of pressure I don't need—and I can't handle it." He also spoke of his envy of other guys at school who could "do things" with their dads. Thus far, there was no male replacement in sight, and he missed it. "Sometimes I get real mad I don't have a dad," he said. "But it's sad, too—how do I know it's not something I did that keeps him away?"

John's fears are not unusual; as we have said before many children feel that they are somehow to blame for their parents' divorce.

The custodial parent in this story could just as easily be the father, with roles reversed. Either way, the situation reveals some of the pitfalls of failing to adequately plan for visitation and then to follow the plan.

When parents begin to define agreed visitation, they should be governed by the general welfare of the child. What are the child's specific needs? What is reasonable for him or her? The child of a divorce in the traditional custodial/noncustodial arrangement has two very general needs: *first*, a need for a consistent and loving relationship in a fixed single parent home; *second*, a need for ongoing contact and a loving relationship with the noncustodial parent. The New York courts have emphasized this factor of the child's need for a continuing relationship with the noncustodial parent. Parents who can manage to put the needs of their children ahead of their own bitterness are more likely to negotiate thorough and successful visitation plans.

DEVELOPMENTAL STAGES OF CHILDHOOD

One wise strategy is to plan a mandatory annual review of the visitation plan to adjust it to the children's needs.

The children's specific needs change and redefine themselves as they develop through the different stages of childhood. Parents should be ready to adapt the visitation plan periodically to suit these various maturation stages. If a divorced family is flexible, it can accommodate the changes on its own or with the help of a mediator. It should rarely have to resort to the legal system.

Each child passes through six general developmental stages on the way to adulthood. These may be identified as: infant, toddler, preschooler, early elementary, later elementary, and adolescent. An understanding of the needs of each developmental stage will help you design your own visitation plan. The following descriptions are by no means exhaustive, but they will serve to better identify these stages:

Infant (0–1): The infant needs consistent physical care and the ability to develop and bond with at least one nurturing adult. From this consistency the infant will develop security. The infant child should not be made to deal with long absences.

Toddler (1–3½): Toddlers continue the bonding relationship to the nurturing adult. They are learning to understand limits and to assert their own wishes against those of the parent.

Preschooler (3½–5): Children of this age are ready to expand the limits of their world. They may spend longer periods of time away from the nurturing adult. They achieve this expansion by developing relationships with other children either in preschool, daycare, or the neighborhood.

Early Elementary (5–9): Children in elementary school are developing the ability to deal with their communities. Friendships with peers become more important. They are starting to develop a sense of ethics and of confidence in themselves as responsible individuals.

Later Elementary (9–12): Children of this age are becoming increasingly independent. They are taking more responsibility for matters that affect them. The peer group is of great importance.

Adolescence (12+): Younger adolescents require more guidance than older children. In this group, children need to be allowed to make decisions for themselves. Adolescents must be made to feel that their parents trust and respect them.

Based upon the developmental stages described above, the chart at right might be a reasonable *minimum* visitation plan in a situation where there is no shared responsibility through joint physical custody.

COMMON VISITATION SOLUTIONS

Divorcing parents who wish to go beyond the indefinite "reasonable visitation" provision commonly obtain provisions along the following lines in their decrees:

WEEKENDS

Times and dates should of course be varied to fit the needs of the child and parents:

> Ordered, Adjudged, and Decreed that husband shall have visitation with the child on every other weekend, from Friday at 6:00 P.M. through Sunday at 6:00 P.M., commencing Friday, January____, 19__.

An alternative provision might provide:

> Ordered, Adjudged, and Decreed that husband shall have visitation with the child on the first, third, and, if applicable, the fifth weekend of each month from 9:00 A.M. Saturday through 4:00 P.M. Sunday, commencing Saturday, January____, 19__.

HOLIDAYS

Parents must carefully consider how holidays are to be divided. Keep in mind the child's needs as well as your own. After all, how many turkey dinners can a child eat on Thanksgiving?

AGES		
0–1	Frequency: Length of time: Extended visits:	Twice per week. 2–4 hours. Not recommended.
1–3½	Frequency: Length of time: Extended visit:	Once or twice per week. Daytimes only; 4–8 hours at age 1; phase into overnight (24 hours) by age 3. Not recommended
3½–5	Frequency: Length of time: Extended visits:	Once per week if daytimes; twice per month if overnight. One overnight; 24–32 hours. Up to 2 weeks.
5–9	Frequency: Length of time: Extended visits:	Twice per month. Full weekends. Up to 6 weeks; telephone contact as initiated by child.
9–12	Frequency: Length of time: Extended visits:	Same as ages 5–9. Same as ages 5–9. Same as ages 5–9; Additional times if requested by child, or less time if child requests.
12–14	Frequency: Length of time: Extended visits:	Same as ages 9–12. Same as ages 9–12; child may opt not to have an occasional visit or to change the times. Same as ages 9–12.
14 and over		Visitation to be determined between child and non-custodial parent.

First list the national, local, religious, and school holidays. Holidays extending the weekend into three days should be considered when planning the normal alternate weekend visitation schedule. Though not considered legal holidays, Father's Day and Mother's Day, as well as the respective parent's birthdays, are often included in visitation schedules, as well. Single-day holidays might be handled in this manner:

> Ordered, Adjudged, and Decreed that the father shall have visitation with the child on alternate legal holidays, Father's Day, and father's birthday. Holiday visitation will commence at 9:00 A.M. and continue until 7:00 P.M., except that if birthday visitation occurs during a school day this visitation will commence one-half hour after the child arrives home from school and continue until 9:00 P.M.

The parents may prefer to identify the specific holidays to be spent with the non-custodial parent. For example, they would substitute New Year's Day, President's Day, and Labor Day for "alternate legal holidays."

If the parents determine that holiday visitation should be alternated yearly, inserting the words, "in even-numbered years" will switch the holidays each year. The same principles apply to Jewish religious days.

EXTENDED VISITATION

It is particularly important that long-period visitations be handled well from the very first experience. Christmas, spring, and summer school vacations deserve careful planning. The non-custodial parent has the benefit of a longer visitation with the child and the burden of the longer term responsibilities of caring for the children. This parent will be confronted with the day-to-day tasks assumed by the custodial parent. These responsibilities might include carpooling, daycare arrangements, enrichment activities, and an increased food budget. These temporary lifestyle changes require forethought and planning if the visitation experience is to be successful.

A broad provision covering Christmas and spring school recesses might provide:

> Ordered, Adjudged, and Decreed that the father shall have visitation for a period of one week during the child's Christmas school vacation, the said week to begin at _____ o'clock __.m. on the first day that school recesses and end at _____ o'clock __.m. seven days later in odd numbered years. In even numbered years this visitation shall begin at _____ o'clock __.m. on the eighth day before school reconvenes and ends at _____ o'clock __.m. on the day before school reconvenes.

This provision assumes that visitation is to be alternated yearly. If Christmas and spring visitations are to be for regular periods each year then the reference to "even-/odd-numbered years" should be eliminated. If visitation occurs in the last half of a school vacation, it is wise to allow the child to return home a day before school reconvenes. This gives the child some time to readjust before resuming school activities.

Christmas poses many problems for parents. Parents who celebrate Christmas want to share the package opening experience with their children. This special event might be divided on the basis of Christmas Eve/Christmas Day as follows:

> Ordered, Adjudged, and Decreed that the father (mother) will pick up the child at 9 A.M. on the 24th day of December of each year and return said child at 9 A.M. on the 25th day of December of each year.

The summer visitation usually lasts from two to eight weeks, depending upon the age of the children, the distance to the noncustodial parent's residence, and the employment requirements of each parent. To permit both parents to plan their own summer schedules, a notice provision should be included. A typical provision provides:

> Ordered, Adjudged, and Decreed that the father shall have the child for a period of fourteen consecutive days during the period of June through August, upon thirty days written notice to the custodial parent. When the child attains ten years of age, the summer visitation shall be increased to a period of twenty-one

consecutive days and to thirty consecutive days, when the child attains the age of fourteen years.

CHECKLIST FOR A COMPREHENSIVE VISITATION PLAN

Comprehensive visitation plans include many provisions. You might want to consider all of the following in drafting your visitation schedule:

1. Include a clause specifying that the custodial parent will continue to reside in a particular geographical area.
2. Prepare a clause establishing provisions in the case that either parent moves away. This might require that the parents reach agreement on any move beforehand, and in case of failure to agree, that the issue shall be arbitrated.
3. Include a clause providing for free access between parent and child during times of illness.
4. Prepare a clause preserving specific visitation rights between the child and his grandparents.
5. Make provisions for the noncustodial parent to attend school conferences.
6. Include a clause that the noncustodial parent be made aware of the child's participation in recitals, demonstrations, and sporting events.
7. Include a clause stating that in the event of death or serious incapacitation of one parent, custody shall vest wholly in the other parent.

You may not wish to include all of these provisions, of course, but they indicate the way in which you should try to look into the future and anticipate possible problems.

MAKING YOUR VISITATION PLAN WORK

Once you have drafted a visitation agreement, you have to make it work. The change from being a live-in parent to being a visiting parent creates a new and very vulnerable relationship. If the child and the noncustodial parent have always shared a close bond, there will be additional pain beyond the emotional strains already created by the divorce.

With some foresight, there are ways to minimize the burden of adjustment wherein you build a new relationship with your children. Effort should be made not to make the changes too rapidly. A "go-slow" pattern is especially crucial to the adjustment of very young children.

Each parent has the benefit of knowing far into the future when and where they will be seeing the child. The very young child has a different sense of time, and may perceive an absence of a few days as abandonment. That child needs special attention during the transition to the new custody arrangement. If, for example, the noncustodial parent is to visit only on Saturdays, it will be better for the parent to visit every evening for awhile, and gradually taper off to the weekend provision. Similarly, if your agreement allows you to take the child overnight, it may be advisable to defer the overnights and begin with short, frequent visits to your new home. A very young child may be unnecessarily upset by being forced to spend the night in totally strange surroundings. Eventually, the young child will be confident enough for regular extended visits there. But don't rush it.

It will help if your children have a place of their own at your new residence—somewhere for their own beds and belongings. This will reassure them that they have a permanent place in your new life.

If your children are older, you may wonder what to do on your first few visits. These may be awkward times for you, especially if you are not already close to your children. Some parents make the mistake of perceiving the visit as an occasion for mandatory entertainment. They expect, subconsciously or otherwise, that excursions to the zoo or sporting events help to compensate the child for what he or she has suffered during the divorce. This concept, frequently called the "Disneyland Daddy" phenomenon, may lead the child to have an artificial view of the place, in the child's life, of the parent he/she is visiting, and undermine the establishment of a strong relationship between parent and child.

Children need *fun time* and *work time* with each of their parents. Avoid planning your visits only around "field trips." After all, you will have to talk *sometime*. Both of you need time free from distractions in which to examine your feelings about the divorce and get to know each other in a new way. We have repeatedly witnessed the great satisfaction that blossoms between the noncustodial parent and his child when the "entertaining" stops and they have the opportunity to discover a far stronger relationship. The relationship simply flourishes once they attempt to stay home, talk, and work together.

The presence of more than one child complicates conversation. If you have two children, you and your ex-spouse must consider whether each visit will include both children or will alternate, with each child visiting separately. This requires careful thought from both parents. You will need to consider the needs of the children and their relationship. If they do not get along well, this will be a factor in deciding how to arrange your visits.

Whether you have one or several children, you should recognize that once your visits are established, it will be good for your child to invite a friend along occasionally. This will vary your experience together. It is also very important that your child's friends meet and get to know you. In so doing, you will share more fully in each other's lives.

After settling into your visitation routine, you may find that the agreed-upon weekly, or perhaps less frequent, visits are unsatisfactory to both you and your children. This is particularly true if you have had a close, happy relationship. This will be a lonesome time for all of you. You miss the children and they miss you. You will all benefit if you maintain contact in additional ways. Daily phone calls may be one answer. You may also want to write notes to the children and encourage them to write to you. Additional means of communication can go a long way toward easing the pain of separation. George Newman's book, *101 Ways to be a Long Distance Super-Dad,* is full of good ideas for maintaining communication in these circumstances.

VISITATION RULES FOR PLAYING FAIR

To help you and your spouse minimize difficulties in living with visitation, the following guidelines should be heeded:

NONCUSTODIAL PARENT

- If you have no prearranged schedule for visits, always give fair notice of an intended visit.
- Do not keep the children out too late; stick to the agreed-upon hours.
- Do not make an appointment to see your child if you do not plan to keep it. Your child needs to be able to rely on you.
- If you must cancel a day visitation, give at least forty-eight hours notice, and at least a week's notice for missing a multiple-day visitation.

BOTH PARENTS

- Do not use your child to spy on or carry messages to your ex-spouse; do not question the child about the other parent's activities.
- Do not belittle your ex-spouse to the child.
- Be willing to compromise on the timing of visits, especially as your child grows up, as your children have a right to a life and interests of their own.

CUSTODIAL PARENT

- Do not threaten to stop visits if child support checks do not arrive. The court cannot impose this sanction, and your interference with visitation could affect your custody status.
- Do not make excuses to block visits to the other parent. Your child has a right to see the other parent and needs both of you.

Remember, *visitation is a dual right*. It involves each parent's right to share in the life of the child and the child's right to know both parents and to enjoy their companionship. If you and your spouse remember your child's interests, visits will be happier and more beneficial for all.

CHAPTER TWELVE
SELF HELP

CAN YOU do your own divorce? You and your spouse may in fact be able to negotiate the basic terms of a divorce settlement directly, then bring in an attorney to check on whether you've covered the essential issues and to put the agreement into an effective legal document.

While we don't generally recommend it, you also have the right to represent yourself in court and to submit legal papers you have prepared yourself to the divorce court. But if your case is not contested by your spouse and is simple enough so that you can represent yourself, why not go to an inexpensive attorney who does a high volume of divorce work? Let people who know what they're doing get your divorce rather than try to reinvent the uncontested-divorce wheel yourself. Even experienced attorneys sometimes have their uncontested-divorce papers rejected by court clerks in New York for technical inadequacies. The rules change, and the clerks, who know the rules, don't have time to guide you personally through the thicket.

If your spouse refuses to consent to a divorce, or if there are property, support, or maintenance questions that you and your spouse can't agree on, you definitely need help from an experienced attorney. Remember the old joke about the man who treated himself from the medical articles in *Reader's Digest*—he finally died of a typographical error.

DOING YOUR OWN LEGAL RESEARCH

Clients occasionally ask if they can do some of their own legal research. They are encouraged to do so because they become better informed clients in the process. A client who reads the myriad of conflicting judicial opinions that the lawyer must deal with has a better appreciation for the adage that lawyering is an art, not a science. Furthermore, in becoming aware of the legal principles involved, the client acquires a better understanding of his or her own legal situation. Thus, the client is better able to supply the lawyer with the information needed. I have also observed that the better informed a client is, the more willing he or she is to accept the equivocations and disclaimers the lawyer must give, when rendering an opinion on what the court will do in the case in question. Finally, if the matter must go to trial, the client can anticipate the legal issues involved, apply them to the facts of his or her case, and be a more effective witness.

Please do not assume that reading this book and a few cases makes you a matrimonial lawyer. The divorcing spouse needs a professional in his or her corner; some knowledge of the law makes a better client, not a new lawyer. With that limitation in mind, let's look briefly at what you can do.

First, you need access to a law library. It is most convenient to start with your own lawyer's resources, but sometimes limitations of space or time prohibit that possibility. With a little effort, you can find a law library open to the public. In many counties there is one either in or near the courthouse. Law schools have major collections, and some are open to the public. If necessary, you can always consult your telephone directory or call the State Attorney General, the clerk of the local court, or the local public library to locate the resources you need.

DIVORCE LAW: STATUTES, CASE LAW, AND CONSTITUTIONS

The laws that affect your particular divorce come from three sources: statutes, case law, and, to a lesser extent, state and federal constitutions. Statutes are the laws passed by the legislature. Case law consists of the body of law that is created when judges decide cases, and particularly when a trial court's decision is appealed and judges in appeals courts write decisions. Those written opinions define legal principles and the ways in which those principles should be applied to the facts of the case on appeal. The decisions of some trial courts, and those of most appellate courts, are published by the state in case law books and are referred to as "official reports." Most of the officially reported current decisions are also published in a set called the *New York Supplement, Second Series.* Constitutional law, as applied in New York divorces, is based upon legal interpretations of both the United States and the New York State Constitutions.

THE DOMESTIC RELATIONS LAW AND THE POCKET PART

Divorce cases are decided on the basis of (1) specific divorce statutes promulgated by the legislature, (2) more general legal principles, and (3) plain old common sense. Legislative enactments (statutes) are codified by number and then arranged by subject within a multivolume set of books. In New York they are found in the Domestic Relations Law, published as Book 14 of McKinney's *Consolidated Laws of New York Annotated.*

The index for the Domestic Relations Law is located at the end of the two-book set, which together comprise Book 14. Thus, if you have a particular issue you want to research, such as the duty of a mother to provide child support, you would look under "support and support proceedings" and other words that come to mind when checking the index. You will then be referred to specifically numbered statutes bearing upon the subject, which in this case would be Section 32 of the Domestic Relations Law. Following each statute will be a summary of court cases interpreting the statutes. These "annotations," as they are called, are court decisions in which the meaning of the statute has been explained. These court decisions are considered "precedent", which subsequent courts will attempt to follow. If some cases in the annotations appear to be inconsistent, it may be because different facts led different judges to apply the statute differently. When you have located the applicable statute, be sure to check the small supplement tucked into a pocket inside the back cover of the volume. This "pocket part" is periodically (usually annually) replaced to update the divorce volume. It reflects changes in statutes and later court decisions. In our child support example, you would be misled if you did not check the pocket part, for the law has been amended to make mothers equally liable with fathers for support of their children since the hardcover *Book 14* was printed.

CASES: NEW YORK SUPPLEMENT

After you have read the statutes, reviewed the annotations, and checked the pocket part for changes in the law or later cases, you will want to make a list of those cases bearing on the issue you are researching. To read these written decisions, you must then turn to the "official reports," or more likely in your library, to the *New York Supplement*.

Finding the decisions you wish to read is simple. The citations in the annotations are nothing more than abbreviated titles of cases. Thus the citation to *Friederwitzer v. Friederwitzer,* 447 N.Y.S.2d 893, means that the case is found in the 447th volume of the second series of the *New York Supplement,* beginning at page 893. Be careful to distinguish between the first and second series of the *New York Supplement.* If you want the second series, look for the "2" on the spine of the book.

When you have located the case, you will need to become acquainted with its organizational format, which is in four phases. First, you will see the case number of this court opinion, the names of the judges, and the date of the court's decision. Then, before the actual opinion of the court, you will find numbered annotations, a brief history of the case including lower court decisions, and a summary of this court's decision. Third, you will find listed the names of legal counsel for both parties. Finally, there will be the decision itself.

The numbered annotations, called "headnotes" or "syllabuses," at the beginning of the report are concise principles of law which the *editor* compiling the volume has gleaned from the court decision. *They are not official statements by the court.* Rather, they are an aid to the reader in spotting issues the court has dealt with in the case. The numbers by the headnotes correspond to specific paragraphs in the body of the opinion, and will allow you to quickly turn to the critical part of the case in which you are interested.

SHEPARDIZING

Every week courts decide cases that limit, modify, or overrule older cases. Therefore, there is always a chance that the case that says everything you want has been affected by a recent decision. *Shepards' Citation* is an index devoted to keeping you informed of all recent cases affecting your case. Basically, *Shepards'* picks up every subsequent case report that mentions the case you have just read. By following this research trail, you will locate the most current judicial thinking on the case you originally started with. In the library, you will find that *Shepards'* currently has hardbound volumes for New York case citations up through at least 1980. More recent cases will be *Shepardized* (and found) in paperbound volumes. The most recent cases will be found in newsprint "slip" volumes.

To ensure that the cases you have found pertaining to your issues are still good law, you must *Shepardize* those cases. To do this, you begin with the first volume that includes your case and work your way forward to the most recent slip volume. The *Shepards' Citation* will also list legal periodicals and treatises, where the name of your reported case was mentioned. By reading the introductory pages of *Shepards' Citations* you will soon feel comfortable tracking down and researching these subsequent reports. Good lawyers *Shepardize* every case before using it in court, and if you are going to do your own legal research, you should do the same.

OTHER AIDS

The best aid to understanding New York divorce and family law (and consulting this is perhaps a better idea than reading the statutes and cases yourself) is *Law and the Family—New York*. This is a multivolume treatise written by Henry H. Foster, Jr.; Doris Jonas Freed; and Joel R. Brandes. Annual supplements keep it up to date. It is written for lawyers, but it is lucid, comprehensive, and accurate. It is frequently cited by New York courts. The publisher is Lawyers Co-Operative Publishing Co. of Rochester, N.Y. Other resources for your research include the following:

1. *Nutshells*. These are short, readable volumes by West Publishing Co. on various areas of law from a national perspective. The *Family Law Nutshell* has helped many law students understand family law, and it might help you. *Nutshells* are inexpensive to buy, but can also be found at most law libraries.
2. *Legal Encyclopedias*. These are long, generally thorough sets of books that summarize the state of the law on many subjects, including variations among different states and references to specific cases and other authorities. *American Jurisprudence* (Am.Jur.) and *American Jurisprudence Second* (Am.Jur.2d) are two examples of legal encyclopedias. In New York we have *New York Jurisprudence,* where the relevant sections are under "Domestic Relations."
3. *New York Digest 3rd*. This contains brief summaries of court decisions organized according to the issues of law involved. This can be very useful in helping you find, under the "Divorce" sections, cases that are similar to yours.

CHAPTER THIRTEEN

COHABITATION: LIVING-TOGETHER ARRANGEMENTS

MANY PEOPLE, including divorce survivors, are choosing to live together unmarried in close emotional, sexual, and economic relationships. Gays and lesbians do not have the option of bringing their relationships under the protective umbrella marriage affords. Other couples, though heterosexual, consciously reject marriage for one reason or another. Living-together arrangements are different from marriages in that the state participates neither in the beginning nor in the ending of the relationship. There is no statute with special rules, like those the Equitable Distribution Law provides for married couples, to divide accumulated property once the relationship ends.

We limit our discussion of cohabitation to situations where one partner is economically dependent upon the other during the relationship, or where there is a pooling and sharing of resources. These relationships pose unique legal problems. Traditionally, courts have not been very responsive when one party, often an economically dependent woman, asks for help when cohabitation ends. Sex outside of marriage violated state laws, and the state wanted to discourage cohabitation. But the law follows changing social, political, and economic realities, and cohabitation has arrived as a widely accepted lifestyle in New York and in other parts of the country.

This is why a chapter on unmarried cohabitation appears here, in a book about divorce. It has become such a common domestic arrangement that it demands recognition in a book on the severing of domestic arrangements. The Census Bureau tells us that in 1984 there were about two million unmarried-couple households, up from about one-half million such households in 1970. The bureau's definition of unmarried-couple households is: "two unrelated adults of opposite sex who are sharing living quarters." The great majority of these households probably consist of "cohabitants" as we have defined them.

Even more striking than the fact that all unmarried-couple households increased fourfold from 1970 to 1984 is the fact that unmarried-couple households, where the partners averaged between twenty-five and forty-four years of age increased twelvefold, from about 100,000 in 1970 to about 1,200,000 in 1984.

In addition, the Census Bureau states that in 1983 there were about 750,000 households with only two unrelated male adults and about 500,000 households with only two unrelated female adults. It is difficult to estimate how many of those couples are gay cohabitants as defined above, but the figure is probably several hundred thousand.

LIVING TOGETHER: THE PROS AND THE CONS

Relationships are made more of feelings than of facts, so any decision to marry or live together should be based primarily on the feelings of each party. The legal protections of marriage are not needed by every heterosexual couple. However, no one should decide against marriage and for cohabitation without being well informed of the legal consequences.

Marriage laws protect the rights of parents regarding access to their children, the rights of children to support from the parents, and the rights of spouses to be compensated for their financial and emotional investment in their relationship. In addition, married couples are given: (1) preferential income, gift, and estate

Cohabitation: Living-Together Arrangements

tax rates; (2) different social acceptance for themselves and their children; (3) insurance coverage for the death or injury of the other spouse; and (4) rights to the other party's estate, even if there is no will bequest, and also to survivorship benefits from pensions and similar sources.

Living together may provide a couple more freedom and flexibility to craft a long-term relationship, particularly if one partner has a strong feeling, from experience or abstract conviction, against marriage. Cohabiting may require more work than marriage, but some parties claim that it makes for a more exciting, vital relationship. Also, many couples use cohabitation as a trial period before marriage. We personally recommend to many clients who have gone through divorce that they try living with the new true love for awhile before tying the knot. This is not illegal in New York, assuming both parties are presently unmarried; however, if one party is still someone else's spouse, such a living-together arrangement is technically adultery, which is both a crime and a ground for divorce in New York.

An explicit, written living-together agreement is most appropriate where each party has good capacity to bargain with the other over personal and family needs. Relationships where one party consistently dominates the other are philosophically less suited for living-together agreements because the legitimate needs of the weaker party may not be stated or met, though much the same thing can be said for marriage. When parties have close-to-equal bargaining strength, or where the party with greater strength uses it to create an agreement that works for both parties, the results can be quite satisfying. As one of our clients described it:

> "It works because we're even and very careful. I've got an income, she's got an income, and we've both got property and the sort of respect that comes from knowing that each of us can go it alone if we have to. No kids though, as we agreed to get married if it came to kids."

This couple has lived together for almost ten years. They drew up a careful contract taking care of expenses and incomes and agreed to renegotiate it every year. In their words:

"So far it's been great. Of course we've had our fights and arguments, but there's *something about not being legally bound* to stay together that makes this relationship so special. Being able to go anytime gives us the freedom to come home each day because we *want to*. Sure, we've both thought about leaving lots of times, but we get over the anger. This may sound weird, but being able to think about leaving makes it much easier to choose to stay."

PROMISE ME ANYTHING BUT PUT IT IN WRITING

New York, under the Court of Appeals 1980 decision in *Morone v. Morone,* 429 N.Y.S.2d 592, will enforce clear and definite oral or written agreements between cohabitants, *even though* the agreements give the cohabitants some economic rights and obligations similar to those the law gives to married couples. *Morone* involved an alleged *oral* contract to share accumulated property. There are obvious difficulties in proving at a trial that there were conversations in which the parties agreed to divide property accumulated during cohabitation. It is the word of one against the other. Both cohabitants need the protection of a written agreement. A financially dependent cohabitant who takes care of the parties' home needs assurance that she will not be left penniless after years of being a homemaker. A wealthier cohabitant needs protection from exaggerated or fabricated claims for support or property division.

The *Morone* court said that New York has power to enforce oral agreements, in which the parties clearly agreed to divide assets accumulated during cohabitation, or in which one cohabitant agreed to support the other financially. The deal cannot include compensation for sexual services the cohabitants supply each other. The *Morone* decision said that New York courts cannot infer a contract for property division or other compensation from the facts of a couple's living together like husband and wife.

Morone's rejecting the idea that cohabitants could get contract rights just from living together in a marriage-like relationship meant that Ms. Morone had to convince a court that

Mr. Morone made clear promises to her to share property in return for her domestic services. If she failed to prove such conversations with Mr. Morone, she would not get any of the property Mr. Morone accumulated in his name (but through the couple's joint efforts), even though the Morones had lived together for twenty-three years and had produced and reared two children. Moreover, she could not qualify for either wife support or maintenance, which are reserved for spouses only under New York law. In New York, and perhaps all states, "palimony"—alimony for a nonmarried cohabitant—does not exist because support and alimony rights are based on statutes that cover only spouses.

The wealthier partner also has uncertain rights and obligations under merely verbal contracts. How is an attorney to predict how successful a client's present heterosexual or gay lover may be in convincing a court, after the relationship has turned sour, that broad financial promises were exchanged in *conversations* during cohabitation? In that type of lawsuit, the client will probably find that his version of the oral promises exchanged differs markedly from his ex-lover's.

At least four states, including California under *Marvin v. Marvin,* 557 P.2d 106 (1976), do enforce "implied" contracts for division of property accumulated during cohabitation, or for payment for services rendered. A court in California may therefore infer an enforceable contract from the conduct of an unmarried couple in living together as if married. Whether a California court will infer a contract for a given couple, and what its terms will be, depends on the facts of the individual case, including the reasonable expectations of the parties. Michelle Marvin ended up without any recovery after the celebrated and prolonged *Marvin* litigation. The law constantly changes, and perhaps New York cohabitants will be able to prove and enforce contracts implied from cohabitation when and if *Morone* is extended. That possibility is another reason to put down *in writing* just what cohabitants expect of each other now and in the event the relationship ends.

SAFETY FIRST: ISSUES FOR A LIVING-TOGETHER AGREEMENT

Once the need for a cohabitation agreement is established, what should go into it? Basically, everything that the parties would want in a prenuptial agreement were they marrying instead of cohabiting. The exception is that the written contract should not mention any sexual expectations the cohabitants have of each other. Not even New York or California, certainly among the more socially liberal states, will enforce a contract that is "meretricious" in Webster's sense of explicitly involving payment for sexual services.

Try to draft as much of the contract as you can on your own. Once you have done so, check with a lawyer who is experienced in this area. Like a medical exam, a small investment now could save you a much bigger one later.

Although each arrangement should reflect the unique needs of the parties, there are some elements that may be common to most such agreements:

Separate property. What property will be held separately? How will it be managed in the event that the owner is incapacitated?

Common property. What portion will each party own of each shared property? How will purchase costs be shared? How will the payments, maintenance, and other responsibilities be shared? How will properties be divided if the relationship breaks down?

Separate income. What incomes will be considered separate? How will such income be managed by each party, and what will be done in the case that either party is temporarily or permanently incapacitated? Should each party give the other a strong power of attorney, allowing the other to conduct his or her affairs during incapacity?

Common income. What specific income or portions of income sources are to be shared? What living expenses and other uses will this shared income be used for, and how will such income be managed in the event that one party is disabled?

Modification, review, and termination of the agreement. How often will the agreement be updated, and how will it be modified? Will parties seek legal advice to insure that the modifications are valid? When and how can the agreement be terminated?

And for heterosexual couples:

Children. What will they be named? What provisions will be made for their education? How will paternity be acknowledged? How will they be supported in the event of a breakup or the disability of one of the parents?

Marriage. Will the agreement terminate if the parties decide to marry, or will portions of it carry over?

These are but a few of the concerns that should be addressed in a comprehensive living-together agreement. Each couple has unique circumstances which create unique legal problems that should also be addressed. The space limitations of this book do not allow more elaboration at this point; but this chapter plus your own research should allow you to put together a basic agreement that you can then submit to a lawyer for refinement. Remember that doing your own work does more than save you legal fees. It provides you with more confidence to manage your lives together and an agreement that better reflects the uniqueness of your relationship.

STATUTORY COMMON-LAW MARRIAGE: NOT IN NEW YORK

Many states have statutes providing that couples who live together and hold themselves out to the community as husband and wife have a legally-binding common-law marriage, even though there has never been a wedding. New York has not such a statute since 1933. However, as of this printing, common-law marriage still exists in Alabama, Colorado, Washington, D.C., Georgia, Idaho, Iowa, Kansas, Montana, Ohio, Pennsylvania, Rhode Island, South Carolina, and Texas. If you and your partner lived together in one of these states, check with a lawyer to see if that state considers you married under common law. If you are married under the laws of any state, New York will recognize you as married here.

YOUR PROPERTY: HOW IT CAN BE OWNED

Generally, the law provides three basic forms of ownership that determine the disposition of property (in the absence of a contract) when the relationship breaks up. These are sole title, tenancy-in-common, and joint tenancy.

> *Sole title* ownership occurs when the title to the property is taken in one name only. When the relationship ends, the property will end up in the possession of the cohabitant whose name is on the title. Even if both cohabitants contributed to the property, either by purchasing it with joint funds or by providing services, the law sometimes will not protect the non-titleholder.
>
> *Tenancy-in-common* (or cotenancy) describes the situation where property is held by more than one person. Here, each person's name is on the title to the property and cohabitants would have an undivided one-half interest in property they own together. If one party dies, his or her half goes into his or her estate.
>
> *Joint tenancy* differs from tenancy-in-common in that it includes the right of survivorship. Thus, if one cohabitant dies, the surviving joint tenant or tenants get all the property. If there are four joint tenants, the one who lives the longest would get everything.

Thus, tenancy-in-common or joint tenancy are means of insuring that you will get your investment back when the relationship breaks up. Under either arrangement, each cohabitant can ask a court to divide the property and give each cohabitant his or her one-half interest. Sole title owners can convert to tenancy-in-common or joint tenancy, but this requires a conveyance of the sole owner's interest to both of them. This transaction can create tax consequences, so you should consult a lawyer before attempting it.

INHERITANCE AND YOUR PROPERTY

Persons who live together have no automatic rights of inheritance from their partner's estate. One solution is to make a will giving your cohabitant partner what you want him or her to have if you die. Particularly if you have significant properties, your will should be drafted and executed with care.

Mistakes and ambiguities invite conflict and court battles between your partner and your relatives, who may feel that living together does not create a strong claim to your money. If this happens and you have not made an adequate will, your relatives may succeed in preventing your partner's claim to any of the property you have shared. There is the example of one couple who had lived together and shared their earnings for forty years before one party died. Neither had written a will, so the surviving partner lost almost everything to his partner's family because title to all the property was in his partner's name.

CHILDREN: TO ABORT, TO ADOPT, OR TO KEEP

In January 1973, the United States Supreme Court held that the right of privacy included the right of a woman to decide whether or not to terminate her pregnancy before the fetus became viable. Abortion is legal under certain circumstances, and the rules depend upon when it is done during the pregnancy. That court later held that physicians do not have to perform requested abortions, but it did strike down a variety of regulations imposing unreasonable or unduly restrictive licensing regulations on doctors performing abortions. It also held that neither a husband nor a father has a right to withhold consent. Minors, under certain circumstances, have the right to seek abortions without parental consent. The "right to life" debate continues and is beyond the scope of this discussion. But whether and under what circumstances an abortion would be appropriate is an issue that some couples may treat in their cohabitation agreement.

If abortion is not an option, adoption may be an answer if the cohabitants have an unwanted pregnancy. The legal procedure for adoption is not complex. Unlike abortion, the father may withhold his consent and thus bar the adoption. A 1972 United States Supreme Court decision held that the interest of a man "in the children he has sired and raised, undeniably warrants deference and . . . protection." As a consequence, New York has laws requiring that the father be notified of the intended adoption.

Parenthood without marriage creates even more, and somewhat different, problems than parenthood with marriage. The first concern is to legally establish paternity. The surest way is for the father to sign the birth certificate and to get a court declaration of paternity. You also will want to protect your child's rights in case you die. It is important for you to make adequate provision for your child in your will and to name him or her as a beneficiary for adequate insurance or other death benefits.

A child born to cohabitants is entitled to support from both parents just as though the child had been born in lawful wedlock, and punishment for nonsupport is similar to that in the marriage situation.

Adoption by cohabitants, particularly gay cohabitants, can be difficult, perhaps more difficult than for a single parent. Some caseworkers who evaluate prospective adoptive parents regard cohabitants as less stable than single parents. The caseworkers fear the child could be harmed by the breakup of the adoptive parents, and, for heterosexual couples, question why the couple's commitment to each other has not led to marriage.

LIVING WITH ANOTHER DURING DIVORCE: THE RISKS

Most states make adultery a crime, but rarely enforce the law. Except in pure no-fault states, adultery is a common ground for divorce. Moreover, in some states, if you openly live with a person awaiting a divorce, you risk being sued for alienation of affections. New York, however, has done away with the alienation-of-affections cause of action. It is clear that persons not yet divorced who live together are, to some extent, compromising their divorce case even though a criminal prosecution is extremely unlikely. Often the other spouse grows hostile and uncooperative when he or she discovers the cohabitation arrangement. That hostility could frustrate the entire divorce negotiation process.

Post-divorce custody and maintenance provisions can be affected by a cohabitation arrangement. New York statutes permit the modification of a prior court order awarding maintenance, if there is a living with and a holding out of another man as husband. Also, cohabitation may open questions of whether the parent's current living arrangement is suitable for children from his or her former marriage.

CHANGING YOUR NAME: CHANGING YOUR CREDIT

Name changes can be granted to either cohabitant. The only statutory prohibition is that the change of name must not be designed to defraud. You need only go through a simple court procedure. By adopting your mate's name you may affect your credit rating; creditors may lump it together with that of your partner. Children born of unmarried parents historically were given their mother's surname. Now they may take the father's name as well. This can be accomplished by his written consent, by adoption, or by a paternity suit. Remember, however, that any of those options also gives the father significant rights, should the mother later wish to have the child adopted by a third person.

THE DILEMMA OF INSURANCE

Cohabitants have difficulty insuring each other because most insurance companies require that the person buying the policy have an "insurable interest." Some insurance companies will not allow one cohabitant to insure the life of the other because they have no "interest" in each other. Moreover, it may be difficult for an unmarried individual owning life insurance on his or her own life to name his or her cohabitant as beneficiary upon death, because the class of persons you can name as beneficiaries is also limited by law.

Insurance companies can avoid their obligations by claiming fraud in the application. Thus, if you put down your cohabitant as your "wife" for beneficiary purposes the company can claim a breach of contract, alleging that they would have declined to issue the policy if they had known that the beneficiary was not legally your wife. You may have to shop long and hard to find a company that will insure you for the benefit of your cohabitant. Be certain that you are candid with the information you furnish the insurance company, lest you lose the entire policy.

The children of these relationships also have problems with insurance. In order to have an insurable interest in the life of their father, these children must show that he acknowledged them and that they relied upon him to some extent for support.

Other kinds of insurance policies are also difficult for cohabitants to obtain. Although the usual homeowner's insurance policy has a clause that protects the other residents of the household, this is usually construed to mean members of the insured's family. The same is true of medical and hospitalization insurance. People who live together do not yet have the same "dependency" relationship even though the child is certainly dependent upon his father! No legal spouse may well mean no insurance. As with life insurance, if you lie to get coverage for your cohabitant, you may lose your benefits.

SOCIAL SECURITY

One of the few legal benefits of cohabitation is social security. Senior singles who have already earned their social security benefits can live together and still collect two checks. If they marry, these double payments end. A cohabitant cannot collect social security from a partner's account after the other's death. The children of these relationships, however, do derive benefits through both parents. Note that a deceased and unmarried worker-father must be established officially as the child's father either by court order or by proven acknowledgment. In addition, the worker must have been living with the child at the time of death or been contributing to his or her other support and the child must have been entitled to inherit under the law of the state where they resided.

TAXES: THE EXTRA COST OF COHABITATION

Despite the 1982 and 1984 "reform" amendments to the United States tax code and the Tax Reform Act of 1986, taxes remain a key source of confusion and anxiety for many people. This is especially true for cohabitants because they are denied many benefits received by married couples in income, estate, and gift taxes; for example:

1. Cohabitants must file separate returns and may pay more taxes on their two individual returns than a married couple with the same income would pay on a joint return, particularly where only one party has significant income.
2. Any payment for companionship from one cohabitant to the other could be taxed as "compensation for services."
3. Cohabitants must pay gift tax on major gifts given to each other. Gift tax is waived for gifts between married people.
4. Each cohabitant will be taxed for annual gifts to other persons over $10,000. A husband and wife may pool their exemptions so that one or the other may give $20,000 per year to a third party without having to pay a gift tax.
5. Upon death of a cohabitant, property passing from one cohabitant to the other is subject to estate tax. Upon death of a spouse, property passes to the other with significant estate tax exemptions.
6. When cohabitants end their relationship they will be subject to income and capital gains tax for dividing their property. When spouses divorce and divide their property they are less subject to income tax.

LEGISLATION: A BETTER FUTURE FOR COHABITATION

Clearly, cohabitants cross a minefield of legal problems. New York has solved some of these problems with *Morone* and other cases. Further change in this area, however, may require legislation. This legislation, from our viewpoint, should give adults who choose to form long-lasting cohabitation relationships, whether gay or heterosexual, and perhaps to raise children, protections and controls similar to those that New York now provides to married people. Such legislation must be very carefully drafted and create rules for cohabitant property, analogous to those now provided for marital property. It is unlikely, however, that such legislation will be enacted in the near future.

Personally, we recognize and accept that many people believe that living together in a sexual relationship without marriage is morally wrong. Our position is simply that, while people are free to make such moral judgments, the state should not abandon its concern for fairness and justice. We see no adequate reason why the housekeeping partner in a sensitive and productive long-term cohabitation relationship should not be given protections similar to those the housekeeping partner in a long-term marriage now receives. The argument that the housekeeping partner deliberately chose to live "a life of sin," and should be punished for that immoral conduct, has little appeal when so many couples are living together without marriage.

CHAPTER FOURTEEN
CONCLUSION

THE NATURE of families and the nature of family law have changed significantly over the past ten years of the authors' divorce practice. Joint custody is now common, and the law gives increasing protection to new family forms such as cohabitants, stepfamilies, and single-parent families. Our law must protect children's best interests regardless of the family form chosen by their parents.

Our goal in writing this book has been to provide the reader with an understandable and relevant manual for humanizing the divorce process. This book would not have been possible without the criticisms and personal stories offered by earlier readers. Future editions will incorporate your suggestions, stories, and concerns. If you have comments, suggestions, or criticisms, please write to us at the following address:

> Grier H. Raggio, Jr.
> 10 East 40th Street
> 43rd Floor
> New York, New York 10016

With your help, future editions of this book will continue to address legal and procedural questions, as well as psychological issues critical to families involved in divorce proceedings in New York.

APPENDIX A

HISTORICAL AND POLICY OVERVIEW
by
Henry H. Foster, Jr., and Dr. Doris Jonas Freed

The chapters of *Divorce in New York* are confined to the specific issues involved in current New York divorces, and we consider it useful to explain briefly how New York divorce law became the way it is.

The original *judicial* ground for divorce in New York was adultery. In 1787, Alexander Hamilton, on behalf of a wealthy New York client, succeeded in obtaining the adoption of the adultery ground. Until September 1, 1967, adultery remained the only ground for divorce in New York, although most other states had long since adopted more expansive grounds for divorce.

The strict New York law of divorce imposed by religious and conservative groups led to "escape hatches" from the literal interpretation of the law. One was the bilateral divorce. In the nineteenth century New York began to recognize such divorces, obtained by New York residents in other states or foreign countries. The presence in person of one party in the other state's court and the appearance of the other at least by counsel was required. At the same time, New York refused to recognize *exparte* (or "mail order") divorces granted in other jurisdictions because the state wanted to protect the stay-at-home spouse (usually the wife) from the legal consequences of migratory divorce, including the loss of support.

Another escape hatch was an uncontested divorce at home in New York, which in this century became routine if the party charged with adultery did not bother to show up in court to defend his or her "honor." At the same time, commencing in the 1890s, annulment became a substitute for divorce, and alleged fraud was the most common basis for annulment. Statutes saved the legitimacy of children born of the annulled marriage; alimony and child support could be awarded on the same basis as in divorce cases. In many counties in New York the number of annulments far exceeded the number of divorces and it was highly significant that, as in the case of divorce, nine out of ten annulment cases were uncontested.

Lawyers and judges had found ways to circumvent the strict divorce law on the books, and in actual practice the divorce process, not time in court, was where "the action was at." Negotiations in law offices dominated the picture. "Bargaining leverage" was crucial to the process.

The divorce process has become more and more focused on the rights of husband and wife to share in the joint or individual property of the couple. In 1980, New York made major changes in the division of property in a new law called the Equitable Distribution Law. The economic incidents of divorce before the Equitable Distribution Law help explain the dramatic reform of 1980.

First of all, the Divorce Reform Law of 1966, which became effective the following year, provided additional grounds for divorce in New York and eliminated the traditional defenses which were applicable only to the adultery ground. One of the new grounds was a no-fault ground in the sense that marital misconduct did not have to be proved where it was established that pursuant to written agreement the parties had lived separate and apart for a year or more. This really is "divorce by consent" because the parties when they sign the agreement know a divorce may be readily obtained a year or more later by either party. Since 1967 the "separation" ground has become by far the most common ground for a New York divorce. It should be noted, however, that, off the record, the separation agreement may signify that there will be no contest if either party seeks a divorce on some other ground.

The Legislative Commission (which we assisted with research and drafting) had planned on rewriting New York alimony and marital property law as its next task on the agenda. It was urgent that a fresh look be taken at that area, because divorce had become easier in New York due to the new grounds and the elimination of defenses. The legislature, however, did not extend the life of the Commission.

Independently, in 1970 the authors of this Overview started to research alimony and marital property law, and shortly thereafter the Matrimonial Law Committee of the New York County Lawyers Association, chaired by Julia Perles, Esq., made Professor Foster chairman of a subcommittee to draft a proposed alimony and marital property law. Both the subcommittee and the Committee worked for the remainder of the 1970s on what became the Equitable Distribution Law. There was frequent consultation with key members of the legislature and their counsel. The bill was first drafted in ideal terms; then changes were made in order to gain legislative acceptance. Bills passed in the Assembly during four successive sessions, beginning in 1976. However, it was not until 1979 that favorable consideration was given by the Senate Judiciary Committee, after Senator Barclay had become its chairman. The measure probably would have passed in 1979, but for the belated opposition of a minority who demanded "equal" instead of "equitable" distribution. In June, 1980, the legislature overwhelmingly rejected "equal" distribution and passed the Equitable Distribution Law, which became effective on July 19, 1980.

During this lengthy drive for enactment of the Equitable Distribution bill, minor changes or additions were made at the suggestion of an ad hoc committee of bar organizations, which had been enlisted to back and lobby for its passage. In addition, various legislators as well as counsel to the Governor and for the Senate Judiciary Committee suggested minor changes or additions. Assemblyman Blumenthal and Assemblyman Burrows and his staff were most effective over the long haul in backing a bill which had a chance for passage. The remarkable thing, however, is that during its long incubation period the structure and substance of the Equitable Distribution Law remained intact, with its basic premise that modern marriage was an *economic* partnership, not merely a moral and social partnership. As a corollary to this new concept, the assets produced during the marriage by the efforts of one or both spouses, as well as the moneys spent, constitute the kitty to be equitably divided between the spouses upon divorce. This underlies the New York 1980 Equitable Distribution Statute. It sets a new public policy for New York.

What follows is a brief outline of New York law before and after July 19, 1980.

THE LAW BEFORE JULY 19, 1980 *(THE EFFECTIVE DATE OF THE NEW EQUITABLE DISTRIBUTION LAW):*

1. The only marital property distributable by the Court between the parties was jointly owned property, for example a home in the names of both parties, or joint banking or savings accounts.
2. Property in the name of only one spouse was his/her separate property alone. All too often it would turn out that a devious or ungenerous spouse (usually the husband) had placed title to all assets accumulated during the marriage in his own name, and upon divorce, the nontitled wife was entitled to none of the assets, but was relegated to alimony alone.
3. Alimony could be awarded only to wives, not to husbands.
4. The primary duty to support wives and children was on the husband.
5. A wife found guilty of conduct which was grounds for divorce was barred from getting alimony.
6. Mothers were usually awarded child custody; fathers "reasonable" visitation rights.
7. No insurance coverage could be ordered by a court for the wife and family, unless the husband agreed. If the husband dropped dead suddenly, alimony stopped, and the wife and the family, without other resources, were often forced to resort to welfare.

The Law After July 19, 1980 (*The Effective Date of the Equitable Distribution Law*):

1. The court *must* make an equitable distribution of all marital property when the marriage is *terminated* by divorce or annulment (not in case of a decree of judicial separation which does not terminate the marriage).
2. "Marital" property is defined as all property accumulated during the marriage by contributions or efforts of either or both parties.
3. "Separate" property is defined to include property owned separately by a party before marriage, property inherited or gifted by third parties, and compensation for personal injuries.
4. Legal title is irrelevant.
5. Property exchanged for separate property, as statutorily defined, retains that characteristic.
6. The appreciation in value of separate property is also separate property, except that if the appreciation in value is due in part to the contributions or efforts of the other party, that portion becomes marital property.
7. The parties may by formal written agreement designate what is marital property and what is separate property, before or during the marriage, and opt out of equitable distribution by the court. They can thus practically write their own ticket.
8. The guidelines set forth in the law *must* be considered by the court in making its equitable distribution, and the court must set forth in its decision the guidelines it considered and the reasons for its particular determination.
9. Among the most important factors is factor (6), which requires the court to consider "any equitable claim to, interest in, or *direct or indirect contribution* made to the acquisition of such marital property by the party not having title, including joint efforts and expenditures and *contributions and services as a spouse, parent, wage earner, and homemaker, and to the career or career potential of the other party.*"
10. Where a division of particular property is impractical or burdensome, or where the distribution of any interest in a business, corporation, or profession would be contrary to law, in lieu of equitable distribution, the court may make a "distributive award" to achieve equity between the parties. The distributive award may be payable by a lump sum or payable

by installments, which, hopefully, will not be regarded as in the nature of taxable alimony.

11. Possession and occupancy of the marital home may be awarded, regardless of how title to the home is held; or title to the marital home and its contents may be transferred to one of the spouses alone.
12. The entitlement to maintenance is based upon "reasonable needs" and ability to pay, and ten statutory factors *must* be considered in setting the amount and duration of maintenance. Again, the factors considered and the reasons for decision must be set forth in the opinion of the court.
13. Factor (8) for maintenance repeats factor (6) for equitable distribution and requires that the court consider the nonmonetary contributions of a homemaker.
14. Maintenance is set for a particular period of time, but may be extended if the recipient has not become self-supporting in the interim, or it may be modified upward or downward because of a substantial change in circumstances, including financial hardship.
15. Guidelines for child support are also set forth in the statute and child support is made a mutual obligation of parents, according to their respective incomes and resources, except that the nonmonetary contributions of the custodial parent to the care and well-being of the child must be considered in allocating the burden of child support.
16. The court may order that one party purchase, maintain, or assign an insurance policy covering health and hospital care and related services, to protect the other party and children; and the court may further order the maintenance of life insurance on the life of one ordered to pay child support or maintenance during the period of such obligation, with the other party or children named as irrevocable beneficiaries during that time.
17. Enforcement procedures for the collection of child support and maintenance have been tightened up by the New York Legislature.
18. Other services of the Domestic Relations Law have been made gender neutral. (They apply to men as well as women.)

The above outline constitutes the principal reforms achieved by the Equitable Distribution Law.

Appendix A

We believe that, for the most part, the law is being fairly applied by the New York courts. Unfortunately, there are some cases where in our opinion the law has been too narrowly construed, to the detriment of wives.

By far the most common complaint is from the women's groups who continue to demand "equal" rather than "equitable" distribution. Cases from other states, and New York cases as well, indicate that such a change would hurt more women than it would help, in certain situations. A wife of many years should be entitled to a greater proportion than 50 percent of the marital property, particularly where the husband has the ability to generate substantial new income. Moreover, the Equitable Distribution Law seeks to grant and maintain flexibility for determining what is fair and reasonable in individual cases. The contributions of some spouses are substantial, for others it may be minimal.

The proposed equal distribution presumption could become a rule of thumb which is applied inequitably and automatically. Is it not better to have the court weigh and balance the ten statutory factors and achieve a fair result? It is or it isn't, depending upon your view of judges. It is interesting that in Pennsylvania women's groups wanted equitable distribution because they felt that they could get more that way from sympathetic judges, but in New York, their sisters insist upon equal distribution. Is it possible that the latter want 50 percent as the floor and the sky as the limit? It certainly is human to have such a wish, but should we grant wish fulfillment for such wishful thinking?

Finally, with regard to the agitation for equal distribution, would it not be arbitrary and often unfair to presume that a housewife is entitled to one-half the present value of the husband's business or professional practice? Obviously, such an entitlement should depend upon facts of the particular case, and the extent and value of the wife's contributions and efforts will vary considerably. The present statute, as is, provides the flexibility necessary to achieve equity under the facts of the individual case.

A 1986 amendment (Laws 1986, Chapter 844) to the Equitable Distribution Law, summarized above, restructured the factors for equitable distribution and for setting the amount and duration of maintenance. The most significant change in policy occasioned by the amendment was that the former emphasis upon maintenance, based upon reasonable needs and ability to pay, was shifted to "the standard of living of the parties established during the marriage." This change, obviously, was intended to raise the level of maintenance awards. The latter standard had been considered and rejected as idealistic and unworkable by the lawyers (of both sexes) who had drafted the 1980 statute. Their experience had shown that such an ideal might be achieved only where there was affluence or extreme poverty, because two households could not be maintained as cheaply as one. However, former factor (6) had listed standard of living during marriage as a factor to be considered "where practical and relevant." The 1986 amendment has no such limitations, and no distinction is made between short-term and long-term marriages, or for cases where the parties lived beyond (or far below) their means.

Despite this significant change in policy, it is doubtful that courts will strip former husbands of what they are presumed to need to live in dignity and to continue to contribute support to the separated family. As previously mentioned in Chapter 6 on *Property Division*, three new factors were added for equitable distribution, each of which reflected prior New York decisions, and appear to make no substantive revisions.

The new wording of the factors to be considered in setting the amount and duration of maintenance is another matter.

Former factor (3) was changed to read: "(3) *The present and future earning capacity of both parties.*" This may become an entering wedge for an *equalization of future income* approach to maintenance that fails to distinguish between short and long term marriages and between dependent and self-supporting former wives.

Revised factor (4) now reads: "(4) *The ability of the party seeking maintenance to become self-supporting and, if applicable, the period of time and training necessary therefor.*" This appears to be a backhanded swipe at rehabilitative maintenance as distinguished from permanent maintenance, and to be an attempt to make the latter the norm.

New factor (5) for maintenance has no counterpart in prior law and reads: "(5) *Reduced or lost lifetime earning capacity of the party seeking maintenance, as a result of having foregone or delayed education, training, employment, or career opportunities during the marriage.*" A literal application of this factor would be arbitrary and unjust in so many situations, that it is apt to be ignored by the courts. No set off is contemplated for what the spouse received in return during the marriage, and consideration is not given to who decided on a pure homemaker role, who gave grounds for or sought the divorce, etc.

Factor (9) now reads: "(9) *The wasteful dissipation of marital property by either spouse.*" The term "family assets" was changed to "marital property." The reason for the change is not clear, but it may have been designed to give the non-breadwinner greater control over family pursestrings, as in community property states, where there is joint management of the community.

New factor (10) now reads "(10) *Any transfer or encumbrance made in contemplation of a matrimonial action without fair consideration.*" This new factor is identical to new factor (12) for property distribution, and either restates prior decisional law, or is intended to make this factor considered twice, once for property distribution, and again in determining maintenance.

New factor (11) is identical with former factor (10) and reads: "(11) *Any other factor which the court shall expressly find to be just and proper.*" This is the catch-all provision designed to catch anything overlooked in the preceding enumerated factors. The other prior factors for maintenance are not changed by the 1986 amendment. Our conclusion is that the 1986 amendment was intended to better the lot of dependent spouses (usually wives), but that in seeking that laudable goal, the amendments may prove to be unfair or unworkable.

There is one practical way of reducing the flimflam that goes on in divorce cases, and in law office negotiations. That is to remove marital fault from the Domestic Relations Law of New York. The fact that the marriage is dead, regardless of who killed it, should be sufficient for a legal interment. All states now have such divorce grounds—although in a few, as in New York, both parties must consent.

Although most matrimonial lawyers appreciate that no-fault divorce would be in the best interests of clients, children, and the public, and that marital fault grounds are counterproductive, some insist upon the retention of the status quo, perhaps because they have a vested interest in things as they are. Bargaining leverage lurks in the background. The ability to "hang in limbo" the other party still exists in New York, although it may be a short-lived advantage if the party dangling in the breeze is free to move to an adjoining state. This bargaining leverage, which often is effective in the short run, ordinarily inures to the benefit of wives. Some women lawyers and feminists want to retain this bargaining leverage at all costs, and even some who formerly favored no-fault now campaign against it in order to retain bargaining leverage and unfair advantage.

It is not surprising, and it may be natural, for organized pressure groups and lobbies to seek to retain unnatural but accustomed advantages, without regard to the best interests of children, the public, or themselves. The women's movement, notwithstanding the words of caution voiced by Betty Friedan, has valiantly fought sexual discrimination, but it also fights for special advantage and preferential treatment.

The welfare of children and of the public is overlooked when an issue becomes man against woman, woman against man. For example, men's groups have unsuccessfully opposed urgently needed federal and state reforms to improve the collection and enforcement of court alimony and support orders. They deserved to lose that one. But men's groups have attained a measure of success in pushing for a statutory preference for joint custody. They won in the New York Legislature, only to be thwarted by the success of the women's lobby in obtaining the Governor's veto. Perhaps we need special pleaders for the interests of children and the public, in order to offset the activity and to counter the propaganda of the active men's and women's groups. Unfortunately, such a proposed coalition would have difficulty in gaining the ear of public officials or the media, which already have taken sides on many issues that have other dimensions that are ignored.

New York divorce law changed and, we believe, improved

greatly in the more than twenty years we have been closely involved with it. New York's Equitable Distribution Law is one of the most flexible and fair divorce statutes anywhere. New York still lags behind other states as it so far refuses to authorize true no-fault divorces, where either spouse can get a divorce just by telling a court that the marriage is over; but we are confident of progress on that front. We look forward to further improvements in a body of law that directly affects so many New Yorkers.

APPENDIX B

TEXT: NEW YORK STATE EQUITABLE DISTRIBUTION LAW

THE NEW York Equitable Distribution Law, Section 236B of the Domestic Relations Law, contains many of the basic rules discussed in this book. The text is constantly being interpreted and reinterpreted by New York State courts as they apply the law to specific divorce cases that do go to court. Therefore a lawyer's advice as to the current interpretations of the statute is probably necessary to answer the specific questions in your divorce situation. The problem of interpretation has been further complicated due to the enactment of the 1986 amendments to the Equitable Distribution Law of 1980. Those amendments became fully effective on September 1, 1986 and are included in the text below.

Maintenance and distributive award. 1. Definitions. Whenever used in this part, the following terms shall have the respective meanings hereinafter set forth or indicated:
   a. The term "maintenance" shall mean payments provided for in a valid agreement between the parties or awarded by the court in accordance with the provisions of subdivision six of this part, to be paid at fixed intervals for a

definite or indefinite period of time, but an award of maintenance shall terminate upon the death of either party or upon the recipient's valid or invalid marriage, or upon modification pursuant to paragraph (b) of subdivision nine of section two hundred thirty-six of this part or section two hundred forty-eight of this chapter.

b. The term "distributive award" shall mean payments provided for in a valid agreement between the parties or awarded by the court, in lieu of or to supplement, facilitate or effectuate the division or distribution of property where authorized in a matrimonial action, and payable either in a lump sum or over a period of time in fixed amounts. Distributive awards shall not include payments which are treated as ordinary income to the recipient under the provisions of the United States Internal Revenue Code.

c. The term "marital property" shall mean all property acquired by either or both spouses during the marriage and before the execution of a separation agreement or the commencement of a matrimonial action, regardless of the form in which title is held, except as otherwise provided in agreement pursuant to subdivision three of this part. Marital property shall not include separate property as hereinafter defined.

d. The term separate property shall mean:
(1) property acquired before marriage or property acquired by bequest, devise, or descent, or gift from a party other than the spouse;
(2) compensation for personal injuries;
(3) property acquired in exchange for or the increase in value of separate property, except to the extent that such appreciation is due in part to the contributions or efforts of the other spouse;
(4) property described as separate property by written agreement of the parties pursuant to subdivision three of this part.

e. The term "custodial parent" shall mean a parent to whom custody of a child or children is granted by a valid agreement between the parties or by an order or decree of a court.

f. The term "child support" shall mean a sum paid pursuant to court order or decree by either or both parents or pursuant to a valid agreement between the parties for care, maintenance and education of any unemancipated child under the age of twenty-one years.

2. Matrimonial actions. Except as provided in subdivision five of this part, the provisions of this part shall be applicable to actions for an annulment or dissolution of a marriage, for a divorce, for a separation, for a declaration of the nullity of a void marriage, for a declaration of the validity or nullity of a foreign judgment of divorce, for a declaration of the validity or nullity of a marriage, and to proceedings to obtain maintenance of a distribution of marital property following a foreign judgment of divorce, commenced on and after the effective date of this part. Any application which seeks modification of a judgment, order or decree made in an action commenced prior to the effective date of this part shall be heard and determined in accordance with the provisions of part A of this section.

3. Agreement of the parties. An agreement by the parties, made before or during the marriage, shall be valid and enforceable in a matrimonial action if such agreement is in writing, subscribed by the parties, and acknowledged or proven in the manner required to entitle a deed to be recorded. Such an agreement may include (1) a contract to make a testamentary provision of any kind, or a waiver of any right to elect against the provisions of a will; (2) provision for the ownership, division or distribution of separate and marital property; (3) provision for the amount and duration of maintenance or other terms and conditions of the marriage relationship, subject to the provisions of section 5-311 of the general obligations law, and provided that such terms were fair and reasonable at the time of the making of the agreement and are not unconscionable at the time of entry of final judgment; and (4) provision for the custody, care, education and maintenance of any child of the parties, subject to the provisions of section two hundred forty of this

Appendix B

chapter. Nothing in this subdivision shall be deemed to affect the validity of any agreement made prior to the effective date of this subdivision.

4. Compulsory financial disclosure. a. In all matrimonial actions and proceedings in which alimony, maintenance or support in issue and all support or maintenance proceedings in family court, there shall be compulsory disclosure by both parties of their respective financial states. No showing of special circumstances shall be required before such disclosure is ordered. A sworn statement of net worth shall be provided upon receipt of a notice in writing demanding the same, within twenty days after the receipt thereof. In the event said statement is not demanded, it shall be filed by each party, within ten days after joinder of issue, in the court in which the procedure is pending. As used in this part, the term "net worth" shall mean the amount by which total assets including income exceed total liabilities including fixed financial obligations. It shall include all income and assets of whatsoever kind and nature and wherever situated and shall include a list of all assets transferred in any manner during the preceding three years, or the length of the marriage, whichever is shorter; provided, however that transfers in the routine course of business which resulted in an exchange of assets of substantially equivalent value need not be specifically disclosed where such assets are otherwise identified in the statement of net worth. Noncompliance shall be punishable by any or all of the penalties prescribed in section thirty-one hundred twenty-six of the civil practice law and rules, in examination before or during trial.

    b. As soon as practicable after a matrimonial action has been commenced, the court shall set the date or dates the parties shall use for the valuation of each asset. The valuation date or dates may be anytime from the date of commencement of the action to the date of trial.

5. Disposition of property in certain matrimonial actions. a. Except where the parties have provided in an agreement for the disposition of their property pursuant to subdivision three of this part, the court, in an action wherein all or part

of the relief granted is divorce, or the dissolution, annulment or declaration of the nullity of a marriage, and in proceedings to obtain a distribution of marital property following a foreign judgment of divorce, shall determine the respective rights of the parties in their separate or marital property, and shall provide for the disposition thereof in the final judgment.

b. Separate property shall remain such.

c. Marital property shall be distributed equitably between the parties, considering the circumstances of the case and of the respective parties.

d. In determining an equitable disposition of property under paragraph c, the court shall consider:
  (1) the income and property of each party at the time of marriage, and at the time of the commencement of the action;
  (2) the duration of the marriage and the age and health of both parties;
  (3) the need of a custodial parent to occupy or own the marital residence and to use or own its household effects;
  (4) the loss of inheritance and pension rights upon dissolution of the marriage as of the date of dissolution;
  (5) any award of maintenance under subdivision six of this part;
  (6) any equitable claim to, interest in, or direct or indirect contribution made to the acquisition of such marital property by the party not having title, including joint efforts or expenditures and contributions and services as a spouse, parent, wage earner and homemaker, and to the careeer or career potential of the other party;
  (7) the liquid or non-liquid character of all marital property;
  (8) the probable future financial circumstances of each party;
  (9) the impossibility or difficulty of evaluating any component asset or any interest in a business, coproration or profession, and the economic desirability of retaining such asset or interest intact and free from any claim or

interference by the other party;
- (10) the tax consequences to each party;
- (11) the wasteful dissipation of assets by either spouse;
- (12) any transfer or encumbrance made in contemplation of a matrimonial action without fair consideration;
- (13) any other factor which the court shall expressly find to be just and proper.

e. In any action in which the court shall determine that an equitable distribution is appropriate but would be impractical or burdensome or where the distribution of an interest in a business, corporation, or profession would be contrary to law, the court in lieu of such equitable distribution shall make a distributive award in order to achieve equity between the parties. The court in its discretion, also may make a distributive award to supplement, facilitate or effectuate a distribution of marital property.

f. In addition to the disposition of property as set forth above, the court may take such order regarding the use and occupancy of the marital home and its household effects as provided in section two hundred thirty-four of this chapter, without regard to the form of ownership of such property.

g. In any decision made pursuant to this subdivision, the court shall set forth the factors it considered and the reasons for its decision and such may not be waived by either party or counsel.

6. Maintenance. a. Except where the parties have entered into an agreement pursuant to subdivision three of this part providing for maintenance in any matrimonial action the court may order temporary maintenance or maintenance in such amount as justice requires, having regard for the standard of living of the parties established during the marriage, whether the party in whose favor maintenance is granted lacks sufficient property and income to provide for his or her reasonable needs and whether the other party has sufficient property or income to provide for the reasonable needs of the other and the curcumstances of the case and of the respective parties. Such

order shall be effective as of the date of the application therefor, and any retroactive amount of maintenance due shall be paid in one sum or periodic sums, as the court shall direct, taking into account any amount of temporary maintenance which has been paid. In determining the amount and duration of maintenance the court shall consider:

(1) the income and property of the respective parties including marital property distributed pursuant to subdivision five of this part;
(2) the duration of the marriage and the age and health of both parties;
(3) the present and future earning capacity of both parties;
(4) the ability of the party seeking maintenance to become self-supporting and, it applicable, the period of time and training necessary therefor;
(5) reduced or lost lifetime earning capacity of the party seeking maintenance as a result of having foregone or delayed education, training, employment, or career opportunities during the marriage;
(6) the presence of children of the marriage in the respective homes of the parties;
(7) the tax consequences to each party;
(8) contributions and services of the party seeking maintenance as a spouse, parent, wage earner and homemaker, and to the career or career potential of the other party;
(9) the wasteful dissipation of marital property by either spouse;
(10) any transfer or encumbrance made in contemplation of a matrimonial action without fair consideration;
(11) any other factor which the court shall expressly find to be just and proper.

b. In any decision made pursuant to this subdivision, the court shall set forth the factors it considered and the reasons for its decision and such may not be waived by either party or counsel.

c. The court may award permanent maintenance, but an

award of maintenance shall terminate upon the death of either party or upon the recipient's valid or invalid marriage, or upon modification pursuant to paragraph (b) of subdivision nine of section two hundred thirty-six of this part or section two hundred forty-eight of this chapter.
7. Child support. a. In any matrimonial action, or in an independent action for child support, the court as provided in section two hundred forty of this chapter may order either or both parents to pay temporary child support or child support. Such order shall be effective as of the date of this application therefor, and any retroactive amount of child support due shall be paid in one sum or periodic sums, as the court shall direct, taking into account any amount of temporary child support which has been paid. The court shall not consider the misconduct of either party but shall make its award for child support after consideration of all relevant factors, including:
   (1) the financial resources of the custodial and non-custodial parent, and those of the child;
   (2) the physical and emotional health of the child, and his or her educational or vocational needs and aptitudes;
   (3) where practical and relevant, the standard of living the child would have enjoyed had the marriage not been dissolved;
   (4) where practical and relevant, the tax consequences to the parties; and
   (5) the non-monetary contributions that the parents will make toward the care and well-being of the child.
   b. In any decision made pursuant to this subdivision, the court shall set forth the factors it considered and the reasons for its decision and such may not be waived by either party or counsel.
8. Special relief in matrimonial actions. a. In any matrimonial action the court may order a party to purchase, maintain or assign a policy of insurance providing benefits for health and hospital care and related services for either spouse or children of the marriage not to exceed such period of time as such party shall be obligated to provide maintenance, child support or make payments of a distributive award.

The court may also order a party to purchase, maintain or assign a policy of insurance on the life of either spouse, and to designate either spouse or children of the marriage as irrevocable beneficiaries during a period of time fixed by the court. The interest of the beneficiary shall cease upon the termination of such party's obligation to provide maintenance, child support or a distributive award, or when the beneficiary remarries or predeceases the insured.

b. In any action where the court has ordered temporary maintenance, maintenance, distributive award or child support, the court may direct that a payment be made directly to the other spouse or a third person for real and personal property and services furnished to the other spouse, or for the rental or mortgage amortization or interest payments, insurance, taxes, repairs or other carrying charges on premises occupied by the other spouse, or for both payments to the other spouse and to such third persons. Such direction may be made notwithstanding that the parties continue to reside in the same abode and notwithstanding that the court refuses to grant the relief requested by the other spouse.

c. Any order or judgment made as in this section provided may combine any amount payable to either spouse under this section with any amount payable to such spouse as child support or under section two hundred forty of this chapter.

9. Enforcement and modification of orders and decrees in matrimonial actions. a. All orders or decrees entered in matrimonial actions shall be enforced in the manner provided by law. The court may, and if a party shall fail or refuse to pay maintenance, distributive award or child support the court shall, upon notice and an opportunity to the defaulting party to be heard, require the party to furnish a surety, or order the assignment of wages, or the sequestering and sale of assets for the purpose of enforcing any award for maintenance, distributive award or child support and for the payment of reasonable and necessary attorney's fees and disbursements.

b. Upon application by either party, the court may annul or

Appendix B

modify any prior order or decree as to maintenance or child support, upon a showing of the recipient's inability to be self-supporting or a substantial change in circumstance, including financial hardship. Where, after the effective date of this part, a separation agreement remains in force no modification of a prior order or decree incorporating the terms of said agreement shall be made as to maintenance without a showing of extreme hardship on either party, in which event the decree or order as modified shall supersede the terms of the prior agreement and decree for such period of time and under such circumstances as the court shall determine. Provided, however, that no modification or annulment shall reduce or annul any arrears which have been reduced to final judgment pursuant to section two hundred forty-four of this chapter. Any other arrears accrued prior to the making of such application shall not be subject to modification or annulment unless the defaulting party shows good cause for failure to make application for relief from the judgment or order directing such payment prior to the accrual of such arrears. Such modification may increase such maintenance or child support nunc pro tunc as of the date of application based on newly discovered evidence. Any retroactive amount of maintenance, or child support due shall be paid in one sum or periodic sums, as the court shall direct, taking into account any temporary or partial payments which have been made. The provisions of this subdivision shall not apply to a separation agreement made prior to the effective date of this part.

APPENDIX C

PREPARING FINANCIAL INFORMATION FOR YOUR LAWYER

Time is what a lawyer sells, and the more background work you do on your case, the less time you will need to buy from your lawyer. Your efforts to prepare your own background and financial information will save you money and make you a fuller participant in a process that is important for your future.

TAKING CHARGE

In addition to saving attorney fees, the process of committing your assets and liabilities to paper is a learning experience. This exercise is consistent with our belief in involving the client fully in the divorce process. It is a particularly valuable experience for dependent spouses, who frequently have little experience with the family finances. For the first time, they are required to account for the tangible assets and liabilities present in their marriage. This mastery of the facts provides such spouses some measure of control over what is happening to them. Although we recognize that many divorcing clients feel they cannot cope with the arduous task of filling out a family budget, it is well worth the effort. In fact, completing this difficult task as best you can is really an investment in the future: almost invariably, *those who take control at this point are better able to solve post-dissolution problems without the aid of a lawyer.*

THE BACKGROUND QUESTIONNAIRE

The aftermath of a divorce includes the creation of two households where one previously existed. That means that the same family incomes and resources will now have to stretch to serve two homes. The information below is necessary in order to assess the financial impact of the divorce on your future lifestyle.

Furnish this information for both spouses, not just yourself. Unlike a medical history, a legal history involves three parties: you, your spouse, and the entity that you are about to dissolve, the marriage. The lawyer needs to know details, sometimes even intimate and embarrassing details, about all three entities to do a good job.

Here are blank questionnaires for your own use:

A. General Background

	WIFE	HUSBAND
1. Birthdate		
(a) Age now		
(b) Age when married		
2. Date of marriage		
(a) Place (city)		
(b) County		
(c) State		
3. Extent of education		
4. Vocational skills		
5. List when such skills last used		
6. Religion		
7. State all health problems since marriage		

(a) List doctors
currently seen   _____   _____
(b) List medications
currently taken   _____   _____

B. Employment, Earnings

	WIFE	HUSBAND
1. Employer	_____	_____
(a) Address	_____	_____
(b) Telephone number	_____	_____
(c) Job title	_____	_____
(d) Length of employment	_____	_____
(e) Work Schedule	_____	_____

2. Information regarding family income from all sources
   (a) List gross income for past 3 years (attach copies of tax returns; if unavailable, copies of W2 Forms)

   $_____ $_____
   $_____ $_____
   $_____ $_____

   (b) *Present annual gross* wage or income (attach pay stubs for last 2 pay months): $_____ $_____

   (c) Other present and projected income, *annual,* including comissions, bonus, rentals, real estate contracts, pension, profit sharing,

Appendix C

disability, unemployment or sick leave benefits, interest, public assistance, social security, dividends, child support.

Identify source   1) $ _____   1) $ _____
                   2) $ _____   2) $ _____

(d) Projected *annual gross* income: total items 2(b) and 2(c)

	TOTAL GROSS:	TOTAL GROSS:
1983	$ _____	$ _____
1984	$ _____	$ _____
1985	$ _____	$ _____

(e) Projected *annual* reductions from *gross* income
  (1) FICA SS   1) $ _____   1) $ _____
  (2) Federal, State & City Income Taxes (# of dependents)   2) _____   2) _____

Mother's Children From Prior Marriage

	Name	Birthdate	Age	*Present Custodian*
(1)				
(2)				
(3)				

Father's Children From Prior Marriage

	Name	Birthdate	Age	Present Custodian
(1)				
(2)				
(3)				

Are any children handicapped or disabled?   Yes No
If yes, indicate which child and detail problem.

Are any children adopted?   Yes No
If yes, indicate if by stepparent or other.

LIVING EXPENSES: A MONTHLY BUDGET

Most of us have never made a budget, much less lived within one. However, spiraling inflation makes budget planning just economic good sense. The hard facts of a divorce demand that you start planning your future living expenses *now*. You may want to consult a financial planner.

To prepare a monthly budget, start reviewing your check register or canceled checks. If you pay by cash or credit for most household expenses, start keeping receipts. Even if you pay by check you will be surprised at the number of items purchased with cash or credit, so do not forget to factor in these outlays too. The following form, will help you prepare your budget.

In answering budgetary questions, calculate your expenses for the future, after separation. Take into account whether you or your spouse will have custody of the children. Calculate the children's expenses as if they will be living primarily with you, if that is a real possibility.

C. MONTHLY EXPENSES

1. Housing
    Rent, mortgage and cooperative/condominium
        payments $_____
    Installment payments for improvements $_____
    Installment payments for furniture, appliances $_____
    Repairs, gardening, household help,
        miscellaneous $_____
    Taxes & insurance (if not included in mortgage
        payments) $_____
    Other: _____ $_____
                                     TOTAL HOUSING $_____

2. Utilities
    Heat (gas & oil) $_____
    Electricity $_____
    Water, sewer, garbage $_____
    Telephone $_____
    Other: _____ $_____
                                     TOTAL UTILITIES $_____

3. Food and Supplies
    For_____ persons $_____
    Supplies (paper, tobacco, pets) $_____
    Meals eaten out $_____
                         TOTAL FOOD & SUPPLIES $_____

4. Children
    Babysitter $_____
    Clothing $_____
    Special health care or treatment not included in
        paragraph (6) below $_____
    Lessons, sports, clubs, camp $_____
    School expenses (not tuition) $_____
    Tuition (if any) $_____
    Haircuts, personal expenses, allowances $_____
                 TOTAL EXPENSES OF CHILDREN $_____

5. Transportation
    Vehicle payments or leases $ _____
    Vehicle insurance & license $ _____
    Vehicle gas, oil, ordinarly maintenance $ _____
    Vehicle repairs—identify $ _____
    Parking, tolls $ _____
    Taxi or public transportation $ _____
                        TOTAL TRANPORTATION $ _____

6. Health Care (omit if fully covered)
    Insurance $ _____
    Uninsured dental expense $ _____
    Uninsured medical expense $ _____
    Uninsured eye care expense $ _____
    Uninsured drugs, prosthetics, etc. $ _____
                        TOTAL HEALTH CARE $ _____

7. Personal Expenses for Self
    Clothing (include credit card payments) $ _____
    Dry cleaning $ _____
    Cosmetics, toiletries $ _____
    Clubs, recreation $ _____
    Education $ _____
    Books, newspapers, magazines, photos $ _____
    Gifts $ _____
    Vacations $ _____
    Other: _____ $ _____
                        TOTAL PERSONAL $ _____

8. Miscellaneous
    Life insurance $ _____
    Court-ordered support or maintenance
        (Identify beneficiary of such payment) $ _____
    Savings and Pension Payments $ _____
                        TOTAL MISCELLANEOUS $ _____

9. Debts (not included above)

Creditor	Amount	Monthly Payment

TOTAL MONTHLY DEBT PAYMENTS $ _____

10. TOTAL MONTHLY EXPENSES
    (ITEMS 1–9) $ _____

PROPERTY: LISTING AND VALUING

The next major area to explore with your lawyer is property distribution (see Chapter Six, "Property Division"). To advise properly, the lawyer will need to be adequately informed about *all* your assets and liabilities. When listing and valuing your property, try to be as specific as possible. The hardest part of this will be placing a valuation on each item. We have included some methods to help you with this task. For example, to find the present market value of your home, enlist the aid of a realtor. He or she will be happy to evaluate your home in the hope of acquiring your listing if you choose to sell. A commonly used source for valuing vehicles is the *N.A.D.A. Official Used Car Guide* or "blue book," which is published monthly and is available through most automobile dealerships and some public libraries. An insurance adjuster can give you a more accurate value of your car than a car dealership, as they use additional sources for valuing a car, such as the "gold book" and the *Cars of Particular Interest (CPI) Book*. A few telephone calls should give you an idea of the current value of your vehicle, but physical inspection is the only reliable method for determining your car's actual value. The same methods apply to boats and trailers. In some cases you may need to check with your banker or insurance agent.

Property Inventory

1. **Family Home**
   - (a) Address _____
     City, State, ZIP _____
   - (b) Date of Purchase _____
   - (c) Purchase Price $ _____
   - (d) Down Payment $ _____
   - (e) Source of down payment _____
   - (f) Monthly payment $ _____
   - (g) Current mortgage balance $ _____
   - (h) Present market value $ _____
   - (i) Present annual taxes $ _____

2. **Other: List details as above**
   Vacation property _____

3. **Real Estate Investment Property (raw land, condo, summer home, etc.)**
   - (a) Owned in partnership with _____
   - (b) Date of purchase _____
   - (c) Purchase price $ _____
   - (d) Down payment $ _____
   - (e) Monthly payments $ _____
   - (f) Taxes $ _____

4. **Automobiles owned including motorcycles and recreational vehicles**

Year	Make	Market Value	Amount Owed	To Whom	Who Uses

5. Boats and trailers

Year	Make	Market Value	Amount Owed	To Whom	Who Uses

6. Furniture and Appliances*

Room	Item	Balance Owing	Market Value
		$	$
		$	$
		$	$
		$	$
		$	$
		$	$
		$	$
		$	$
		$	$
		$	$
		$	$
		$	$
		$	$
		$	$
		$	$
		$	$
		$	$
		$	$
		$	$
		$	$

*Be sure you do not place too high a value on your home furnishings. A good measure of an item's value is what you would probably get for it at a "cash only" garage sale and *not* the item's retail price or the replacement value.

7. Unusual Items: antiques, stamps, coins, sporting equipment, club memberships, other

Item	Date Acquired	Price at Acquisition	Current Market Value	Balance Owed and To Whom	Who Uses

8. Life Insurance

Face Amount	Company	Type of Policy, Number	Person Insured	Benefits	Cash or Loan Value	Out-standing Loan

9. Bank Accounts

Name of Bank	Branch	Type of Account	Current Balance	Who May Withdraw	Name	Date Open

10. Stocks, Bonds, Commodities, Margin Accounts

Name	Number of Shares	Purchase Price Per	Current Price	Total Current Value	If Bond, List Current Value

11. Certificates of Deposit

	1.	2.	3.
Face amount	_____	_____	_____
Maturity date	_____	_____	_____
Where located	_____	_____	_____
Interest	_____	_____	_____

12. Loans and Other Debts

	Security Deposits	Earnest Money	Loans	Promissory Notes	Mortgages and Contracts
Amount					
Owed by Whom					
Due When					

13. Pension, retirement, profit sharing

	WIFE	HUSBAND
(a) From whom		
(b) Your contribution		
(c) Company contribution		
(d) State if vested or not		
(e) If not vested, years to go before vested		
(f) Lump sum entitled to now		
(g) Monthly amount entitled to		
(h) Date and age when entitled		
(i) Current age		

Business Valuation: A business may appear to be worth nothing since almost all profits are consumed by salaries. Salaries do, however, help determine the value of the business. In any event, you will probably need a Certified Public Accountant or an appraiser to find out exactly what the business is worth. The company's most recent financial statements would help this process along.

14. **Do you or your spouse own or operate a business?**
    Yes _____ No _____
    (a) Name: _____ When Started: _____
    (b) Were you married then? Yes _____ No _____
    (c) Is it incorporated? Yes _____ No _____
    (d) If yes, total no. shares outstanding: _____
    (e) How many shares do you own? _____
    (f) How many shares does your spouse own? _____
    (g) Are you or your spouse an officer? Yes _____ No _____
        If yes, indicate who and which office: _____
    (h) How many employees in business? _____
    (i) Net worth (latest quarter or last year): _____
    (j) Profit or loss made last year: _____ Last quarter: _____
    (k) Where are the books kept? _____

15. **Did you help to provide your spouse with an education?**
    Yes _____ No _____

    (a) If yes, list when: _____
    (b) What education was received: _____
    (c) If you worked then, your monthly take-home pay: _____
    (d) If your spouse worked, his or her monthly take-home pay:
    (e) The source of each of your incomes: H _____
                                             W _____

16. **Have you or your spouse completed any financial statements or loan applications:**
    Yes _____ No _____
    Date made: _____
    For whom: _____
    Present location: _____

17. **Have you ever signed an agreement that altered the ownership rights between you and your spouse (e.g. marital or separate property agreement)**
    Yes _____ No _____
    Date: _____
    Where located: _____
    Reason for agreement: _____

Appendix C   201

18. Have you ever signed a guarantee or indemnification agreement, making you or your spouse liable, in the event another breaches that agreement?

    Yes _____ No _____

    When signed: _____
    For whom: _____
    If in defualt: _____
    Amount guaranteed: _____
    What security was given? _____
    State where agreement located: _____

19. When you married did you give up social security, alimony (maintenance), retirement?

    Yes _____ No _____

    (a) If yes, list what you gave up: _____
    (b) Monthly amount received: _____
    (c) How long would you have received it? _____
    (d) Can you get it back? _____

20. Separate Property: Any property that you or your spouse

    (a) owned at the time you married: _____
    (b) received through inheritance: _____
    (c) received as a gift from someone other than spouse: ____
    (d) acquired after agreement was executed, or divorce action begun: _____

21. If you own such property, list and describe it below:

List Property	Date Acquired	Balance Owed at Time of Marriage	In Whose Name Is Title Held	How Acquired

22. If you contributed separate property to the marriage, list what property that was, when you contributed it, what the value is, and why you contributed it to the marriage: _____
_____

KEY DOCUMENTS: A CHECKLIST

You can shortcut some of the questions posed in this appendix by supplying your lawyer photocopies of various documents. As a general rule, all documents that tend to establish ownership of assets, existence of debts, and current income should be assembled and made available. To begin, you should gather the following documents:

1. Federal income tax returns for the last three years
2. Last three pay stubs for both spouses that show deductions from gross pay
3. Your current check register (which tends to establish your spending patterns)
4. The most recent annual statement of pension or retirement benefits furnished for each spouse
5. Savings passbooks
6. Certificates of deposit, Treasury bills, and the like
7. Financial statements given to a banking institution in connection with a recent loan
8. Monthly or quarterly bank statements for all checking and savings accounts
9. Charge card (Master Charge, Visa, American Express, etc.) statements for the last few months
10. Warranty deeds, contracts, title insurance, and other documents establishing ownership to real estate, such as, your home
11. Title certificates and registration statements for cars, trucks, recreational vehicles, boats, etc.
12. If a business is owned, the most recent tax return, annual profit and loss statement, and most current monthly or quarterly profit and loss statement
13. List of all current debts, monthly payments, and reason for the debt
14. Each employer's annual statement describing medical/life insurance benefits and profit sharing plans, etc.

The list could go on and on. Use your own common sense to assemble those documents that you feel would be pertinent during your first or second interview with the lawyer. Your lawyer will be able to guide you further as you proceed.

APPENDIX D

EXCERPTS FROM GOVERNOR CUOMO'S 1986 PROPOSED CHILD SUPPORT FORMULA BILL

(c) Child support formula: In order to determine the amount of child support, the court shall apply the child support formula as follows:

(1) Determine the income of both the custodial and the non-custodial parent.

(2) Subtract the non-custodial parent's self-support reserve (proposed as $5,590 for 1986 -ed.) from his/her income to give the non-custodial parent's marginal income.

(3) Subtract the custodial parent's self-support reserve from his/her income to give the custodial parent's marginal income.

(4) Add the non-custodial parent's marginal income to the custodial parent's marginal income to arrive at the combined marginal income.

(5) Divide the non-custodial parent's marginal income by the combined marginal income to find the non-custodial parent's share of the combined marginal income.

(6) Refer to the table in paragraph (d) of this subdivision representing the appropriate number and age of the children to be

supported. Find the combined marginal income as determined in subparagraph four of this paragraph on the selected table. Find the dollar value and percentage which appear in the row representing the combined marginal income as determined in subparagraph four of this paragraph. Compute the support obligation required for the combined marginal income selected. Where the children to be supported are in different age categories, the support obligation shall be calculated for each age and weighted accordingly.

(7) Multiply the non-custodial parent's share of the combined marginal income as determined in subparagraph five of this paragraph by the amount computed in subparagraph six of this paragraph.

(8) Add to the figure calculated in subparagraph seven of this paragraph, ten percent of the non-custodial parent's self-support reserve.

(9) The sum arrived at in subparagraph eight of this paragraph shall constitute the annual support obligation of the non-custodial parent except as increased pursuant to subparagraph ten of this paragraphh. When the sum derived in subparagraph eight is less than six hundred dollars the annual obligation shall equal six hundred dollars, unless increased pursuant to subparagraph ten of this paragraph.

(10) Where the custodial parent is working or receiving elementary or secondary, or higher education leading to employment, or vocational training and incurs child care expenses as a necessary result thereof, reasonable child care expenses shall be prorated in the same proportion as the non-custodial parent's income is to the total parental (non-custodial and custodial) income. The non-custodial parent's pro rata share of child care expenses shall be added to the previously determined support obligation to determine the total yearly support obligation.

(d) Child support obligation tables:

Appendix D

TABLE 2A

Support Obligation on Combined Marginal Income:
Two Children, Age 0 to 11

Combined Marginal Income	Support Obligation			
Up to $10,000	33.8% of amount			
$10,001 to $15,000	$3,380 plus	16.7%	of excess over	$10,000
$15,001 to $20,000	$4,215	17.7%		$15,000
$20,001 to $25,000	$5,100	17.5%		$20,000
$25,001 to $35,000	$5,975	20.4%		$25,000
$35,001 to $50,000	$8,015	21.2%		$35,000
$50,001 to $100,000	$11,200	13.3%		$50,000

TABLE 2B

Support Obligation on Combined Marginal Income:
Two Children, Age 12 to 21

Combined Marginal Income	Support Obligation			
Up to $10,000	41.8% of amount			
$10,001 to $15,000	$4,180 plus	20.5%	of excess over	$10,000
$15,001 to $20,000	$5,205	22.7%		$15,000
$20,001 to $25,000	$6,340	21.7%		$20,000
$25,001 to $35,000	$7,425	25.9%		$25,000
$35,001 to $50,000	$10,010	26.6%		$35,000
$50,001 to $100,000	$14,000	17.1%		$50,000

APPENDIX E

LAWYER REFERRAL SERVICES IN NEW YORK

STATEWIDE
Lawyer Referral and Information
   Service
N.Y.S. Bar Association
One Elk Street
Albany, N.Y. 12207
(800) 342-3661 (NYS only)
(518) 463-3200

ALBANY COUNTY
Albany
Lawyer Referral Service
Albany County Bar Association
Albany County Courthouse,
   Rm. 315
Albany, N.Y. 12207
(518) 445-7691

BRONX COUNTY
Bronx
Legal Referral Service
Bronx County Bar Association
851 Grand Concourse
Bronx, N.Y. 10451
(212) 293-5600

BROOME COUNTY
Binghamton
Broome Lawyer Referral Service
Broome County Bar Association
30 Fayette Street
Binghamton, N.Y. 13901
(607) 723-6331

CHEMUNG COUNTY
Elmira
Lawyer Referral Service Info-Line
Chemung County Bar Association
Heritage Park
Elmira, N.Y. 14901
(607) 732-6613

DUTCHESS COUNTY
Pawling
Lawyer Referral Service
Dutchess County Bar Association
81 West Main Street
Pawling, N.Y. 12564
(914) 473-7941

Appendix E

ERIE COUNTY
Buffalo
Lawyer Referral Service
Erie County Bar Association
1758 Statler Bldg.
Buffalo, N.Y. 14202
(716) 852-8687

KINGS COUNTY
Brooklyn
Lawyer Referral Service
Brooklyn Bar Association
123 Remsen Street
New York, N.Y. 11201
(718) 624-0675

MONROE COUNTY
Rochester
Lawyer Referral and Information Service
Monroe County Bar Association
1125 First Federal Plaza
Rochester, N.Y. 14614
(716) 546-2134

NASSAU COUNTY
Mineola
Lawyer Referral Information Service
Nassau County Bar Association
Box 431
Mineola, N.Y. 11426
(516) 747-4070

NEW YORK COUNTY
New York
Legal Referral Service
Assn. of the Bar of the City of N.Y. & N.Y. County Lawyers Assn.
42 West 44th Street
New York, N.Y. 10036
(212) 382-6625

National Lawyers Guild Referral Service
853 Broadway, #1701
New York, N.Y. 10003
(212) 673-4970

Legal Referral Service
New York Women's Bar Association
15 East 40th St.
New York, N.Y. 10016
(212) 889-7873

ONEIDA COUNTY
Utica
Lawyer Referral Service
Oneida County Bar Association
Executive Secretary
505 Mayro Building
Utica, N.Y. 13501
(315) 724-4901

ONONDAGA COUNTY
Syracuse
Lawyer Reference Service
Onondaga County Bar Association
505 State Tower Building
Syracuse, N.Y. 13202
(315) 471-2690

ORANGE COUNTY
Goshen
Lawyer Referral Service
Orange County Bar Association
210 Main Street
Goshen, N.Y. 10924
(914) 294-8222

QUEENS COUNTY
Jamaica
Lawyer Referral Service
Queens County Bar Association
90-35 148th Street
Queens, N.Y. 11435
(718) 291-4500

RICHMOND COUNTY
Staten Island
　Legal Referral Service
　Richmond County Bar Association
　1111 Victory Boulevard
　Staten Island, N.Y. 10301
　(718) 442-4500

ROCKLAND COUNTY
New City
　Lawyer Referral Service
　Rockland County Bar Association
　60 S. Main Street
　Box 371
　New City, N.Y. 10956
　(914) 634-2149

SUFFOLK COUNTY
Ronkonkoma
　Lawyer Referral and Information
　　Service
　Suffolk County Bar Association
　4175 Veterans Memorial Highway
　Ronkonkoma, N.Y. 11779
　(516) 981-1600 or 1603

WESTCHESTER COUNTY
White Plains
　Lawyer Referral Service
　Westchester County Bar
　　Association
　199 Main Street
　Suite 800
　White Plains, N.Y. 10601
　(914) 761-5151

APPENDIX F

SUPREME COURTS OF NEW YORK STATE

ALBANY	Court House	Albany	12207	516-445-7714
ALLEGANY	Court House	Belmont	14813	716-268-5800
BRONX	851 Grd. Concourse	Bronx	10451	212-590-3804
BROOME	Court House	Binghamton	13902	607-772-2248
CATTARAUGUS	303 Court St.	Little Valley	14755	716-938-9111
CAYUGA	Court House	Auburn	13021	315-253-1400
CHAUTAUQUA	P.O. Box 292	Mayville	14757	716-753-4266
CHEMUNG	203-205 Lake St.	Elmira	14902	607-737-2847
CHENANGO	Cnty. Office Bldg.	Norwich	13815	607-335-4573
CLINTON	County G'vt Cntr.	Plattsburg	12901	518-561-8800
COLUMBIA	Court House	Hudson	12534	518-828-7858
CORTLAND	P. O. Box 5590	Cortland	13045	607-753-5003
DELAWARE	P. O. Box 426	Delhi	13753	607-746-2123
DUTCHESS	Court House	Poughkeepsie	12601	914-431-1920
ERIE	92 Franklin St.	Buffalo	14202	716-852-1291
ESSEX	County G'vt Cntr.	Elizabeth Town	12932	518-873-6301
FRANKLIN	Court House	Malone	12953	518-473-6767
FULTON	W. Main St.	Johnstown	12095	518-762-9125
GENESEE	Court House	Batavia	14020	716-344-2550
GREENE	Court House	Catskill	12414	518-943-2050
HAMILTON	Court House	Lake Pleasant	12108	518-648-5411
HERKIMER	Court House	Herkimer	13350	315-867-1186
JEFFERSON	317 Washington St.	Watertown	13601	315-782-9295
KINGS	Montague St.	Brooklyn	11201	718-643-8076
LEWIS	Court House	Lowville	13367	315-376-2414

LIVINGSTON	Court House	Geneseo	14454	716-243-2500
MADISON	P.O. Box 668	Wampsville	13163	315-366-2267
MONROE	Hall of Justice	Rochester	14614	716-428-2020
MONTGOMERY	Court House	Fonda	12068	518-853-3431
NASSAU	Supreme Ct. Blvd.	Mineola	11501	516-535-2966
NEW YORK	60 Centre St.	NYC	10007	212-374-8513
NIAGARA	775 3rd St.	Niagara Falls	14302	716-284-3147
ONEIDA	Court House	Utica	13501	315-798-5866
ONONDAGA	Court House	Syracuse	13202	315-425-2030
ONTARIO	Court House	Canandaigua	14424	716-394-4100
ORANGE	255 Main St.	Goshen	10924	914-294-5151
ORLEANS	County Clerk	Albion	14411	716-589-4457
OSWEGO	Court House	Oswego	13126	315-342-0025
OTSEGO	P.O. Box 710	Cooperstown	13326	607-547-4276
PUTNAM	Court House	Carmel	10521	914-225-3641
QUEENS	88-11 Sutphin Blvd	Jamaica	11435	718-520-3717
RENSSELAER	Court House	Troy	12180	518-270-3711
RICHMOND	County Court House	St. George	10301	718-390-5222
ROCKLAND	Court House	New City	10956	914-638-5387
ST. LAWRENCE	Court House	Canton	13617	315-379-2219
SARATOGA	Cnty. Mncpl. Cntr.	Ballston Spa	12020	518-885-5381
SCHENECTADY	620 State St.	Schenectady	12305	518-382-3220
SCHOHARIE	Court House	Schoharie	12157	518-295-8142
SCHUYLER	100 N. Franklin	Watkins Glen	14891	607-535-2423
SENECA	Court House	Waterloo	13165	315-539-9285
STEUBEN	Putney Square	Bath	14810	607-776-7879
SUFFOLK	235 Griffing Ave.	Riverhead	11901	516-548-3785
SULLIVAN	Court House	Monticello	12701	914-794-4066
TIOGA	16 Court St.	Owego	13827	607-687-0100
TOMPKINS	Court House	Ithaca	14850	607-272-0466
ULSTER	Court House	Kingston	12401	914-339-5680
WARREN	County Center	Lake George	12845	518-761-6429
WASHINGTON	Upper Broadway	Fort Edward	12828	518-747-3374
WAYNE	Court House	Lyons	14489	315-946-4895
WESTCHESTER	County Court House	White Plains	10601	914-285-3800
WYOMING	143 N. Main St.	Warsaw	14569	716-786-3148
YATES	Court House	Penn Yan	14527	315-536-2854

APPENDIX G

RESOURCES FOR DOMESTIC VIOLENCE

N.Y. State Coalition Against
  Violence
Hotline 1-800-942-6906

NYC Victim Service Agency
212-577-7777

For information regarding:
  Shelters
  Counselors
  Legal services
  Techincal assistance

BRONX
  Lincoln Borough Crisis Center
  234 East 149th St., Rm. 21
  Bronx, N.Y. 10451
  (212) 579-5326
  (212) 579-5327

BROOKLYN
  Kings County Crisis Center
  451 Clarkson Ave. CG-56C Bldg.
  Brooklyn, N.Y. 11203
  (718) 735-2424
  (718) 735-2425

BUFFALO
  Community Action Organization of
    Erie County, Inc.
  Family Violence Program
  70 Harvard Place
  Buffalo, N.Y. 14209
  (716) 881-5150 Ext. 215

CANTON
  Renewal House
  3 Chapel St.
  Canton, N.Y. 13617
  (315) 379-9845

CORTLAND
  Aid to Women Victims of Violence
  14 Clayton Avenue
  Cortland, N.Y. 13045
  (607) 756-6363

ISLIP TERRACE
  Long Island Women's Coalition,
    Inc.
  P.O. Box 183
  Islip Terrace, N.Y. 11752
  (516) 666-8833

NYC
Victim Service Agency
2 Lafayette St.
New York, N.Y. 10007
(212) 577-7777

N. TONAWANDA
YWCA of the Tonawanda
  Domestic Violence Program
49 Tremont St.
N. Tonawanda, N.Y. 14120
(716) 692-5643

PLATTSBURGH
Women Incorporated to Aid,
  Educate & Support Women, Inc.
P.O. Box 44
Plattsburgh, N.Y. 12901
(518) 563-6904

QUEENS
Queens Borough Crisis Center—
  Queens Hospital
82-68 164th Street
Queens, N.Y. 11432
(718) 990-3188
(718) 318-3819

ROCHESTER
Alternatives for Battered Women
300 Andrews St.
Rochester, N.Y. 14604
(716) 232-7353

SMITHTOWN
Victim's Information Bureau of
  Suffolk, Inc.
496 Smithtown-by-Pass
Smithtown, N.Y. 11787
(516) 360-3730

SYRACUSE
Vera House, Inc.
P.O. Box 62
Syracuse, N.Y. 13209
(315) 468-3260

WATERTOWN
Jefferson County Women's Center
52 Public Square
Watertown, N.Y 13601
(315) 782-1823

WHITE PLAINS
Mental Health Association of
  Westchester County
Abused Spouse Assistance Services
29 Sterling Avenue
White Plains, N.Y. 10606
(914) 997-1010

Domestic Violence Prosecution
  Unit
Westchester County D.A.'s Office
11 Grove St.
White Plains, N.Y. 10601
(914) 682-2127

APPENDIX H

RECOMMENDED READING ON DIVORCE

The Boy's and Girl's Book about Divorce, by Richard Gardner, M.D. The purpose of this book is to help children get along better with their divorced parents. It was written for children ages 8 to 13, and is intended for reading by children alone or with a parent. A parent could read it to younger children ages 4 to 7. Adolescents will also find much of interest to them in this book. Parents often find this book of great help for themselves, because it is written from the side of the child's thoughts and feelings.

Boy's and Girl's Book About One Parent Families, by Richard Gardner, M.D. This book is a warm guide for children by an excellent author.

Where is Daddy? The Story of a Divorce, by Beth Goff. Written for young children, ages 2 to 5, this book is a read-aloud with lots of drawings. It tells the story of a little girl and what happened to her when her parents divorced and Daddy wasn't there anymore.

Children of Divorce, by J. Louise Despert. This book tells parents in concrete terms how divorce affects children, what to do about it, and where to get help in the doing.

When Parents Divorce: A New Approach to New Relationships, by Bernard Steinzor. This book will help you deal with the fears and anxieties surrounding the breaking up of a home. Dr. Steinzor shows how today's divorces need no longer be surrounded with hopelessness and a sense of loss—and he means this for both parent and child.

Explaining Divorce to Children, edited by Earl A. Grollman. Written for parents and professionals as a guidebook explaining the effects of divorce upon the personality development of a child. This book will teach you how to talk to children about divorce.

Part-Time Father, by Edith Atkin and Estelle Rubin. This book is a guide for the divorced father to help him understand what he will encounter with his children, and how to deal with it.

Mom's House, Dad's House, by Isolina Ricci. This book will help parents to deal with shared custody effectively.

The Kid's Book of Divorce, written by 20 children of divorced families. This book is a child-to-child guide and should be available from your local library.

Creative Divorce, by Mel Krantzler. The focus of this book is on using the crisis of divorce as an opportunity for the growth and development of men and women.

How to Survive the Loss of a Love, by Melba Colgrove, Ph.D., Harold Bloomfield, M.D., and Peter McWilliams. This book provides many hints about ways to allow you to cope with divorce.

Sharing Parenthood after Divorce, by Ciji Ware. An excellent, practical guide to the advantages and disaadvantages of shared custody.

Crazy Time: Surviving Divorce, by Abigail Trafford. A focused effort that examines the emotional conflicts faced by males and females during divorce.

Living with Loss, by Dr. Ronald W. Ramsay and Rene Noorberger.

Marital Separation, by Robert Weiss. A classic sociological work. Heavy reading, but worth the effort.

The Divorced Woman's Handbook, by Jane Wilkie. This book has checklists of things that you must do to make it efficiently through the first year after your divorce.

Don't Say Yes when You Want to Say No (Assertiveness Training Book), by Fensterheim and Baer. An excellent workbook for the intimidated spouse.

Creative Aggression, by Bach and Wyden. A guide to fair fighting.

The Intimate Enemy, by Bach and Wyden. A readable guide that examines our fears of intimacy and deep relationships.

Making Contact, by Virginia Satir. A quasi-academic work on establishing or re-establishing relationships with oneself or others.

P.E.T. Parent Effectiveness Training, by Thomas Gordon. A simple, yet profound guide to parent-child communication.

Passages, by Gail Sheehy. A classic on the life phases of people.

Male Mid-Life Crisis, by Nancy Mayer. A focused inquiry into problems faced by fortyish-aged males, with helpful suggestions for maintaining relationships while growing.

Women in Transition (Feminist Handbook on Separation and Divorce), Women in Transition, Inc. A very encouraging work.

Alone: Emotional, Legal and Financial Help for the Widowed or Divorced Woman, by Antoniak, Scott, and Worcester. A compassionate guide to a difficult period of life.

Women and Anxiety, by Helen A. DeRosis, M.D. A quasi-academic study, but worth the effort.

The Seasons of a Man's Life, by Daniel Levinson. A helpful guide to the life phases faced by men.

Getting Free, by Ginny NiCarthy, M.S.W. The best book we have found for female victims of emotional and physical abuse. Helpful, nonjudgmental, and empowering.

Crisis Time!, by William A. Nolen, M.D. A warm and fascinating autobiography of a successful surgeon who endured a staggering midlife crisis. Dr. Nolen attempts to explain the medical basis for the crisis and offers helpful advice.

Additional copies of *Divorce in New York* may be obtained from your local bookstore, or clip and mail the order form below:

National Book Network, Inc.
4720 Boston Way, Suite A
Lanham, Maryland 20706

Please send me

Divorce in New York

_____ Paperback copies @ $10.95 each $_____

_____ Hardcover copies @ $19.95 each $_____

(Maryland residents add 5% sales tax per copy) $_____

Postage & handling @ $1.50 each $_____

   I enclose check or money order in the amount of $_____
(No cash or COD's please. Allow 4 weeks for delivery.)
(15% discount off per-copy price on orders of 5 or more copies)

Name _____
              (Please Print)
Address _____
City _____State_____Zip Code_____